Plain Talk about Church Growth

Steve Clapp

faithQuest
BRETHREN PRESS
Elgin, Illinois

Plain Talk About Church Growth
Steve Clapp

Copyright © 1989 by Mary Jo Clapp

Cover design by Jeane Healy

Library of Congress Cataloguing-in-Publication Data
Clapp, Steve
    Plain talk about church growth/Steve Clapp
        p.   cm.
    ISBN 0-87178-708-9
    1. Church growth–NorthAmerica.   I. Title.
    BR510.C42   1989
    254'.5–dc20   89-49600
                                CIP
Manufactured in the United States of America

Contents

Contents

1

CAN WE CONTROL CHURCH GROWTH?

*Go therefore and make disciples of all nations, baptizing them
in the name of the Father and of the Son and of the Holy Spirit,
teaching them to observe all that I have commanded you; and lo,
I am with you always, to the close of the age.*
Matthew 28:19-20

John Andrews graduated with distinction from a major Protestant
seminary. He took the responsibility for sharing the Gospel and
nurturing church growth seriously. His first full time charge consisted
of two midwestern churches, located ten miles from each other. One
was actually a "country church" with a membership primarily of
farmers and their families. When John arrived, that church had a
membership of seventy-eight and an average worship attendance of
thirty-seven. The "town church" on his two-point pastoral charge had
183 members and an average worship attendance of seventy. The
town church included in its membership not only farmers but also
teachers, the high school principal, business owners, and some people
who commuted to work in a city thirty-five miles away.

Filled with a recent graduate's zeal for evangelism, John worked
hard to increase membership, average attendance, and financial
support for both churches. While church members initially resisted
his almost constant push for change, his good nature and genuine
affection for them won them over.

When John left four years later to pastor a suburban church, he
could look with pride at his accomplishments. The country church,
faced with a slow but continuing drift of people off the farms, dipped
slightly in membership to sixty-seven. The average worship
attendance, though, went to forty-eight, and the church's program was
better in almost every area. The town church grew to 218 members
and an average attendance of 125. Both churches declined during the
tenure of the next pastor, though John was the first to admit in
correspondence with former members that the increasing problems
of farmers made "holding even" a difficult task for both churches.

John received no increase in pay when he went to the 293 member
suburban church, and the average worship attendance of 150 was less
than the combined average on his two-point charge. John correctly

perceived that this church had enormous opportunities with the rapid growth of the suburb. He and his family spent thirteen years there. At the end of that time, the church had 812 members and an average worship attendance of 368. When John received an excellent opportunity as senior pastor of an urban congregation, his successor in the suburban church had a difficult time. Membership, average attendance, and church program declined slightly during the two years under that pastor; but the next minister reversed that trend.

During John's seven years as pastor of the urban congregation, St. Paul's Church, he often regretted the decision to leave the suburban situation. St. Paul's had looked like a fine opportunity, and John was the youngest senior pastor in the church's history. The church, however, had been in decline for twenty years. Once a proud downtown church with a membership of almost 4,000, St. Paul's had slipped to 2,115 members by John's arrival. John felt the financial resources and program strength of the church were sufficiently great that the decline could be reversed. The community itself was gaining slightly in population, and there were signs that the downtown area was not going to deteriorate as badly as in the recent past.

John's committed leadership inspired the church to undertake an $800,000 renovation program at the start of his third year there. They made a commitment to stay in the downtown location, and the physical facilities badly needed improvement. By the end of John's seventh year, he told his successor that the major remodeling may have been a mistake. In spite of his best efforts, John saw the church continue to lose more members by death and moves than could be added each year. His sixth and seventh years were the best, with net losses of thirteen and twenty-five members respectively. Total membership had declined to 1,548. Ironically, the suburban church which John had left, in spite of small losses the first two years following his departure, had climbed to 1,266 members and had an average worship attendance slightly greater than the downtown church. As John moved into an administrative position in his denomination, he wished in many ways that he had stayed at the suburban church. While motivations and approaches may differ, church growth has continued to be a major concern of almost every major denomination. The so-called mainline churches like the United Methodist, United Presbyterian, United Church of Christ, Episcopalian, and others have almost all experienced serious net losses in membership and average attendance over the past twenty years. The more evangelical Protestant churches have not suffered as significant a decline. Some evangelical churches have experienced noticeable growth, but few have grown as rapidly as they wished.

Most have found it harder to assimilate members fully than to add them to parish roles.

Roman Catholics in the United States have not traditionally spoken a great deal about church or parish growth. Yet the 23 percent decline in average attendance at mass since 1958 is hard to ignore, and the declining number of North Americans willing to commit themselves as priests causes grave concern for the future. In 1984, for the first time in decades, the Roman Catholic Church in North America suffered a 4 percent membership decline. Increasing numbers of priests are now willing to talk with great seriousness about the issue of parish growth.

John Andrews had many gifts for the ministry, and his career movement reflects those gifts. Yet the churches pastored by John were very much the beneficiaries or the victims of the demographics of the particular situations. While the two-point charge achieved some net growth under John's skilled leadership, that was not a growth that could be sustained over a long period. The country church grew in average attendance but lost net membership even under John. The suburban church in a fast growing part of the country was expected to grow and in fact did. The large downtown church declined – in spite of significant efforts to reverse the decline.

Does that mean the quality of ministerial leadership has no impact on church growth or decline? It does not. Many other suburban churches with similar opportunities for growth have failed to grow at all. Most denominations have more than a few churches which were enthusiastically begun to take advantage of tremendous growth potential but which simply did not make it – not even to the size of John's suburban church when he arrived. St. Paul's rate of decline was slowed considerably by the end of John's tenure there, and most church members felt the quality of their program was much greater and the potential for reversing the trend still present.

There are no simple answers to the question of what causes a church to grow or decline. The competence of the church staff, the dedication of the church members, the nature of the community in which the church is located, and the rise or fall of the community population all contribute to the church's growth or decline.

I started with the story of John Andrews (and while the name has been changed, there is a John Andrews whose career has followed almost precisely that shared in this chapter) because it is important to face squarely the complexity of the church growth issue. This approach is not the "last word" on church growth but a genuinely helpful set of perspectives and tools that can be of great practical use in your parish – regardless of your denomination, church location, church size, or personal level of involvement in the church.

Church Growth in North America

The remainder of this chapter, includes observations on where North America now is in terms of church growth and decline. Even f you do not fully agree with these views, you'll find the book easier to understand if you are aware of them. The bias that is seen is generally less destructive than the one that is hidden. This is the particular direction that some research and conversations with church leaders have taken over the last few years. The seven major observations are:

1. **Church growth is more a matter of demographics than most of us want to admit, but some growth is possible in most situations. And only those who know how to respond to favorable demographics can take full advantage of situations with the highest growth potential.** With only a few significant exceptions, the fastest growing churches are those in communities or neighborhoods that are also rapidly growing. Just plopping a new church in a rapidly growing area will not result in growth; hundreds of examples prove otherwise. Committed lay people and talented church professionals must make the most of favorable demographic climates. The task of assimilating new members in a rapidly growing church is difficult, challenging, and *absolutely critical* to the future.

One must compare church growth to population growth in a given area to have an adequate view of how effectively churches are reaching out. If a given community increases by 200 percent in a fifteen year period of time and church membership only increases by 145 percent in that same period, then pride in the rate of growth is not justified. Most denominational officials have been reluctant to take the full implications of this reality seriously. There is a natural temptation to point with pride to those churches that are growing and to urge greater effort in those churches that are in decline. An actual examination of the numbers, in comparison with the community, suggests that many of the supposedly fastest growing churches in the country are not growing as rapidly as the neighborhoods in which they are located. Likewise, some churches in communities experiencing continual decline in population are managing to hold even or make slight increases.

In thinking about your church's potential for growth, take a realistic look at what is happening in the community in which you are located. If your community is growing, then your church should be – at the same or a greater rate.

Most of us find it hard to resist the temptation to use community population decline as a justification for church membership decline. Certainly there are many situations in which just holding even on membership or losing members at a slower pace than the community loses population is cause for at least modest celebration. The hard truth is that there are few communities in which there is not at least limited potential for church growth. According to the latest polls, three out of every ten people in the United States are still not members of a local church. Thus no matter what the relative growth or decline of population in your community, there are almost certainly people who are candidates for church membership.

If you have never done so, look up population figures for the past twenty years for the area served by your church. Compare the percentage of growth or decline in those figures with the percentage of growth or decline in church membership. You'll have a helpful (and often humbling) measure of how you are doing as a community of God's people.

2.   Some clergy and other professionals in the church have personalities or styles of leadership that clearly nurture church growth. John Andrews has such a style. He was popular in all three of the pastoral charges described. In the suburban situation that had great potential for growth, his leadership and personality were a major part of the church's use of that potential. That particular church grew at a slightly faster rate than the community in which it was located. Two pastors of similar denominations in the same suburb with similar physical facilities were not able to maintain such high levels of growth.   To date, however, no successful vaccine has been developed to inoculate all church leaders with those leadership styles or personality characteristics. While leadership styles may be, to some extent, learned and unlearned, personalty traits are another matter.

Further, the styles and characteristics that correlate well with church growth in one situation will not necessarily bring the same response in another. The same traits that were good for growth in the suburban church served by John were not identical to those needed by the larger urban church. While John unquestionably gave good leadership to St. Paul's, a close examination of his track record there suggests that some different approaches could have yielded better results.

We need to recognize the reality that leadership style and personality traits are related to church growth, but we must be careful about over generalizing. Specific people need to be examined in the context of specific situations.

3.   Much of what we call "church growth" has actually been "member swapping." When an American Baptist in Chicago moves to Houston and joins an American Baptist church there, that move contributes to the apparent growth of the church in Houston but not to the general growth of that denomination. When a Lutheran decides to become a Presbyterian, it's -1 for Lutherans and +1 for the Presbyterians – but there is no net change for the kingdom of God.

Many individual churches that have experienced rapid growth have done so at the expense of other churches in their immediate geographical areas. While it may be argued that persons who cross denominational lines will be more active in the new situation (and one at least hopes this is the case), such instances are not adding to the number of unchurched reached.

As increasing numbers of young adults do not have as strong a sense of denominational loyalty as their parents, those young adults will select church homes in a new community based on many criteria besides the denominational identity of the church. Strong outreach efforts and high quality church programming and preaching will reach larger numbers of these people. Strong outreach and high quality programs and sermons should be encouraged, and growth in those churches is cause for celebration.

For all our talk about church growth over the last several years, we are simply not seeing major change in the percentage of persons who are active members of a local church. The latest Gallup polls as of the time of this writing show that only 12 percent of the United States could be termed "highly committed church members," and three out of ten do not belong to a local church. Some denominations experience net increases; some have net decreases. We are still not effectively reaching the unchurched, and we have far to go in deepening the commitment of many who are token church members.

The Billy Graham Evangelistic Organization and other groups skilled in conducting crusades are quick to point out that the persons reached by these crusades are generally persons who have had exposure to the local church before – at least through Sunday school during childhood. Television ministries seem to reach vast numbers of people, but the statistical evidence is that most of these persons were nurtured in a local church and that a very high percentage of them are still active in a local church. These observations are in no way intended as critical of evangelistic crusades or of television ministries. Let's face the reality. We are not doing a good job reaching the unchurched or reactivating the chronically inactive.

4. If we do not find better ways to involve children, youth, and young adults in the local church's life, the situation for the church in North America could be much worse in twenty years. I don't want to make the situation sound worse than it is. On a statistical basis, young people in the church are just as likely to be involved in church activities as their parents. The problem is that part of that activity does come through parental initiative and will not necessarily be maintained when the youth are no longer under the direct influence of their parents. **Only a third of the teenagers in the United States and Canada are currently receiving religious instruction.** Seventy-four percent of Protestant and 82 percent of Catholic teens feel you can be a good Christian and not attend church.

And while young adults (often defined as persons 19-35 years of age) seem slightly more interested in the church than a few years ago, there has been no enormous reversal of the trend of lower participation by persons in that age range. If the habits are not properly instilled and the commitment to Christ not properly won during the teen years, young adults will not necessarily continue in church activity. Virtually every major denomination is deeply concerned about the difficulty of effectively reaching persons in this age range, and that difficulty stems in good measure from our not having done an adequate job when today's young adults were in their teens.

For many decades, churches assumed that young adults who have "fallen away" would resume church activity when they had children ready for parochial school or Sunday school. While there is still some truth in that assumption, it is not nearly as valid as twenty years ago. If the young adults do not return when they have children, their children will not have the religious nurture provided by the church. While that nurture can theoretically happen within the home, it generally does not happen there, and is far less likely to if the parents are not involved themselves in the life of the church.

Thus our programs of outreach to the young are of crucial importance for the future of our churches. We ignore that reality at great peril.

AN EXERCISE. Take a few minutes to estimate the number of persons in each of the following age ranges who would normally be involved in worship activities, Christian education, or youth programs in a given week in your church. Think of these as the "active" members of your parish:

_____ preschool
_____ grades 1-6
_____ junior high & senior high
_____ young adults (19-35)
_____ middle aged adults
_____ older adults (65+)

Now go through the same list. Put a + (plus) sign beside each age range where you feel the number of active members is as large as it should be for your parish and community. Put a - (minus) sign beside each age range where you feel the number of active members is not as large as it should be for your parish and community.

---

5. **The Roman Catholic Church in North America faces especially great challenges with diminished obedience to doctrinal positions, financial problems in parochial schools, and the declining number of parish priests.** The Roman Catholic Church has great strength worldwide and in North America. While it is stronger in some geographical areas than in others, the Catholic Church is the religious preference stated by 29 percent of the United States. That percentage has increased dramatically since 1947, when it stood at 20 percent. The middle and late ninteen eighties show some scattered membership slippage, but the numbers are not alarming. Wthat is alarming is the fact that the percentage attending mass in a given week has declined 22 percent since 1958. A somewhat superficial interpretation of the data would be to say that many people identify with the Roman Catholic Church but that the number actively involved has declined. While it is an oversimplification of the situation today, many Roman Catholic leaders are concerned about the need for fuller involvement of Roman Catholics in parish life.

The number of young Catholics who resist the church's teaching on birth control, divorce, ideal family size, and other areas is of significant concern. A major study by the Center for the Study of American Pluralism, expressed significant concern about the importance of young people in the Catholic Church having positive feelings at the parish level.

On a very practical level, there is increasing evidence that concern about quality parish programs and effective assimilation of members into parish life runs at comparably high levels in Roman Catholic and

Protestant congregations. This should make possible some exciting cooperative programs in the years ahead.

6. **Most "plans" for church growth on the denominational and the local church level simply do not work – or at least not as intended.** Many denominations, regional church judicatories, and local churches set significant goals for church growth – for one year to twenty year periods of time. Most of those plans, unfortunately, do not come to fruition.

A church only grows as someone who is not currently a member of that church decides to become a member. The fact that the denomination at a national level or the church on a local level has set a specific goal for growth has very little to do with whether a person who is not a member of that church decides to become a member. Implementing denominational strategies at the local church level is extremely difficult. Even getting the average member in the pew to cooperate fully with a program initiated by the governing board of a given local congregation can be a difficult task.

Resolutions and plans, no matter how elaborate, enthusiastic, well planned, or carefully initiated, do not automatically result in local church growth. While many factors are involved in people deciding to join a local church, most studies still show that people join a particular church that a friend, neighbor, or relative initially encouraged them to attend or join. With all the variables, **it still comes down to one person inviting another to become involved in some level of the local church.**

The very fact that you hold this book in your hand means that you have the potential to become a key person for growth in your local church. The outcome has more to do with your own motivation and concern than with any local church, judicatory, or denominational program – and certainly more than with anything said in this book!

The other variable which no book or program controls is the continuing influence of God's grace in our lives and in the lives of others. No matter how hard we work, our work is in vain unless we are open to God's presence in our lives and unless God is permitted to become a part of the lives of others.

Church growth, at the root level, is a very simple process – which is precisely why it is so difficult. It involves a willingness by you and me and others like us to reach out with Christ's love. More about this as we continue!

7. **Church expansion efforts motivated primarily by concern for institutional survival do not work well.** Unfortunately, many of our

most enthusiastic efforts at church growth, at every level, come about because we are concerned about surviving as churches. When nonmembers see us coming out of survival motivation, we look as if we are trying to take something from them rather than give something to them. They understandably become suspicious and wonder about the hidden agenda – and our agenda is generally not well hidden.　　　　While we may declare verbally that we are offering people new life in Christ, they often suspect that what we really want is their money in the offering plate and their help in the Sunday school room, church kitchen, or choir. While all those involvements are important for people and generally deepen what they gain from the life of the church, they are not the best approaches to church growth.

Plain Talk

Most of our local churches are far away from their potential in church growth, and that generally holds true whether a given church is at present experiencing growth or decline. I firmly believe that we are at a point when "plain talk" is the best way to proceed. We need to look realistically at our own situations and find strategies that we can carry out in practical ways. We also need to face some common attitudes that impede church growth.

Over a six year period, the question of what factors help and hinder church growth has been central in many personal research projects, visits to local churches, conversations with denominational executives, and workshops with church leaders. It is interesting to identify:

• Traits and styles of clergy and other professionals that correlate positively with church growth – and in what situations a particular set of traits seems most effective.

• Traits and styles of lay members that make them especially effective witnesses for Christ and recruiters for the local church.

• Successful strategies for motivating both professionals and volunteers to take a greater interest in sharing the good news with persons who are inactive in church or nonmembers.

• Ways in which modem secular marketing models can help share the timeless Gospel. We are continuously competing in various ways with the secular world; we should learn all that we can.

• The ways in which deepened spiritual commitment can help lead people into fuller involvement in the life of the church. There obviously should be a relationship between spiritual growth and church growth, but we have not explored that relationship in much depth.

• Effective ways to make positive changes in the perceptions of people about the local church and to encourage people to reach out more warmly to others.

• The reasons for which so many of our apparently well laid plans for church growth simply do not work. We need a better understanding of the role that serendipity and even playfulness should have in the life of the church. We can experience God in serendipity as well as in carefully laid plans.

• The reasons some churches that seemingly demand strong commitment from members seem to grow and grow and why others that demand strong commitment at best hold even.

• The ways in which, up to the limits of my own ability (with the help of prayer and other people) to discern, God is working within, through, around, and in spite of our very human goals and efforts at church growth.

There is much to be learned in these concerns about the church, human nature, and the grace of God. While there is much in the pages that follow that reflects what others have said about church growth, there are also some new perspectives. Statistical information is shared in those instances where it lends strength to suggestions or perspective that should be helpful, but it is not a technical report. not to let this become a technical report. Statistics date a book quickly, whereas most of the strategies that need to be shared are ones that do not quickly become dated.

While much can be gained if this book is read prayerfully and do not shared with anyone, more will be gained if others are involved in study, prayer, and discussion. This is a book of "plain talk." The strength or the uniqueness of this book comes in:

• a thorough grounding in research and in dialogue rather than the simple reporting of one person's opinion.

• provision of an enormous number of suggestions, not because you can possibly implement them all but because you need the freedom to choose those that will work best for your church – and the more that can be examined, the more additional ideas will be generated for you as you reflect on your situation.

• a firm belief in the central importance of changing attitudes and perspectives of church stuff and members if any real growth is to occur. While strategies are important attitudes and commitment are far more important.

I also believe there must be a healthy tension between our own efforts at church growth and the honest realization that we can do nothing on our own. Unless our goals or attitudes are sufficiently worthy that Christ can work through us and with us, then we will either fail to achieve church growth or the growth achieved will not accomplish the purposes we desire. The church is of God, and it will be preserved, nor is it dependent on our very human limitations. Through the years God has worked in many diverse ways to change the hearts and lives of men and women.

Not all that appears to be successful church growth may in fact be advancing the purposes of God. There is no purpose in growth if that growth does not truly bring more people into a vital relationship with Christ and further our individual and collective service of Christ in the world. Some churches that seem to grow very little may in fact through the strength of their witness to human rights and the needs of the alienated within our society bring sufficiently strong witness for Christ that the kingdom of God benefits greatly.

It begins with you, and with me, and with our relationships with Christ.

2

CHURCH GROWTH BEGINS WITH YOU AND ME

I can do all things in him who strengthens me.
Philippians 4:13

CONCEPT: One individual can make a significant difference in the growth potential of a local church. YOU can make a difference in your church.

Many people have come to feel that only highly trained church professionals or very extroverted volunteers can make a significant difference in the membership and attendance growth or decline of a given local church. Yet my own conversations with clergy, lay staff, active church members, inactive members, and nonmembers convince me that anyone who loves Christ and the church can make a significant difference.

In fact my own conversations with people who have chosen not to join a local church (though some of these people nevertheless will indicate a denominational preference in response to national surveys) suggest to me that the stereotyped "witness" or "church caller" may in fact be less effective than some of us who project less self-confidence.

Many people who are inactive in the church or who are not yet members have become very suspicious of many approaches by religious people. Questions like "Are you saved?" and "Do you know the four spiritual laws?" and "Do you know what you're missing by not being in church?" are a sure turn-off for many of the very people we are trying to reach. A low key approach that expresses a genuine desire to know others as individuals and an absolute refusal to in any way use, manipulate, or trick them is far more effective in reaching most people.

Church growth, as indicated in the first chapter, starts at the level of one person who is active in the church reaching out to one person who is not active. Research continues to reinforce this. Between 50 percent and 64 percent of those going to church were first invited by someone they knew. Of those persons who do not go to church, between 54 percent and 75 percent have never been invited to attend church.

This book does not have to go further than you to make a difference. Your own decision to reach out on behalf of Christ and the church can mean a great deal for the congregation to which you belong or which you serve. By God's grace, it may make a far greater difference than you would imagine.

> **CONCEPT: The most important single step you can take as an individual is to invite someone you know, who is not actively involved in a local church, to worship with your congregation.**

Don't worry about the possibility of being told "No." If you are told "No," accept the response and ask someone else. Our egos or self-worth are not on the line when we ask someone to attend church. All that has to be done is to ask if that person has a church home. If not, then invite the person to attend worship. That is all it takes to get started.

There is much more that can be done to increase the likelihood of a person becoming involved in the church, and many of those things will become clear as you continue reading. The starting point is a simple invitation.

Many of us feel uncomfortable about asking people we know to attend church. It's almost as if we would prefer talking to someone whom we didn't know at all; then if we're told "No," the rejection does not seem as personal. We certainly need to ask people we don't yet know on a personal level to attend church. Many of those people, especially over a period of time, will respond favorably to us. But no one is as likely to give you a favorable response as someone you already know. You can ask people in the kind of low key, no pressure way that will leave them and you feeling all right if they refuse your invitation.

> **CONCEPT: Learn to talk favorably about your local church around those who are not part of the congregation.**

All of us are unhappy with some aspects of our local churches. The sermons may seem poorly prepared; the choir may be slightly off key; the youth program may need improvement; the hallways may need painting. Some church members may be very difficult to work with. Such problems should be addressed and corrected when possible, but the conversation should take place within the community of those others who are active in the church and concerned about the church.

Sharing bitter feelings or negative views of the church with persons who are inactive or nonmembers does nothing to increase the likelihood that they will become members. A prominent campus minister, R. Benjamin Garrison, wrote a small book many years ago titled *Portrait of the Church – Wartsand All*. While the institutional church certainly is the visible representation of the body of Christ, it is still a very human institution. No church is perfect. Some are less perfect than others. Our own points of view have a lot to do with how we see the church. Those of us who are active in the church accept it "warts and all," knowing that we can discover the grace of God in the midst of very human activities.

My wife and I have different tastes in religious music. No choir will ever please both of us. I have a deep love for young people and have spent much of my life working successfully with them. I can find areas for improvement in virtually any church youth program – including those which I've personally directed. My temper, which normally stays under control, can quickly be brought to the boiling point by the manipulative, often hurtful ways in which so many churches handle fund raising.

All of these concerns belong in the community of faith. They certainly are out of place in conversation around people who have nothing to do with the church. Sharing those negative perspectives only will convince nonmembers further that they couldn't possibly want to be involved with that kind of organization.

We stay active in the church because many of our basic needs are met by our experiences there. We have affirming experiences with others. We feel that our contributions make a difference. We feel in closer touch with the living power of Christ. We need to share the positive experiences that we have in church with others, so that they understand the church's importance to our lives.

Because of human nature, it is far easier to plant seeds of discontent than of nurture. One especially nasty remark about an experience at church in the presence of someone who is already uneasy about church matters can do far more harm than four or five positive comments will do good.

Be aware of what you appreciate about your church. Let others know of that appreciation in the course of normal conversation. You will be surprised at the difference it makes.

CONCEPT: If you want to make a difference in church growth, whether you are a church professional or a lay volunteer, start making visits to the homes of prospective members.
If you want to make a difference in the level of activity of those

who are already members, share in routine calling on those persons.

Wading through all the volumes on church growth and decline, examining the styles of successful church professionals, looking at the lives of lay people who consistently bring many others into the church, a regular pattern of visitation stands out. For a church professional, it may mean several calls a week. For a volunteer, it may only be one or two calls a week or a few calls a month. But it makes a difference!

Lyle Schaller says it well in the first part of his excellent book *Growing Plans*: "Despite this plethora of creative ideas and programs, the best single approach is still the old-fashioned system of personal visitation."

Dynamic preaching, creative programs, sophisticated direct mail campaigns, television and radio ministries, and a beautiful church building together will do very little for church growth unless accompanied by shoe leather on the sidewalk, knocking on doors, and visiting over coffee (or tea or lemonade or . . .) in living room and kitchens.

Personal visits have considerable impact on reaching potential members. Persons who are in any way "church shopping" are almost always impressed if they receive a call within a few days of their visit to the church. Follow up calls over a period of weeks can turn prospective members into active members.

Calls on those who are already members can help maintain solid levels of activity for some and renew regular attendance for others. Many who drop out of regular involvement in the life of the church do so because of some conflict which has occurred or some slight which has hurt their feelings. A visit in the home does much to help persons with those feelings. While the issue itself may not be discussed, the fact that someone from the church cared enough to visit makes a significant difference.

Chapter seven focuses in more detail on approaches to personal visitation, and the importance of this contact will be shared repeatedly in this book.

WHAT'S IT LIKE? Here are some statements from people about their first experiences calling on prospective members on behalf of the church:

• "I was nervous at first, but the people were so very glad to receive the visit. They were new to the community and were wanting to get involved. I was the only one who had called on them from a church."

• "I made four visits in one night. Two of the families had just visited our worship services, and they were enthusiastic. I had a great time, and I think there's a good chance both of those families will end up members. The other two families hadn't been to our church but were newcomers. One of them was Jewish and had no interest! But that was still an enjoyable visit. The other family was interested, and I'm going to have the pastor call on them."

• "I was worried about knowing what to say. But I didn't need to be. I may have been a little awkward, but the people were very nice. Even those who weren't interested seemed pleased that I'd made the effort to invite them."

CONCEPT: The most important single attitude related to church growth is a genuine interest and concern in others combined with a sincere desire to share the love of Christ and the church.

The best way for us to share Christ's love and the church's love is to come across as genuinely concerned about other people. In the process of visiting with people, especially the first and second times, we should place far more importance on learning about them than in inflicting our agenda on them. A few simple statements about being glad to meet them and glad they visited church (or hoping they will visit church) are sufficient.

The way in which we approach others depends on our individual personalities. My wife feels that I am absolutely extroverted and that visiting with people about the church is easier for me than for her. That may be true. However, I am no more effective at it than she is. Some of the most effective callers and representatives of the church are people who are more introverted. These people are not pushy; help others feel at ease; and come across with a sincerity which may be clearer than that of more extroverted folks like me. In fact those of us who do lots of calling need to use particular care that we do not always talk in the same cliches and stock answers to questions about the church.

It has been said many times that "no person is irreplaceable." In the sense that life keeps right on going if something happens to anyone, it's true. On the other hand, we were created as unique human beings by a loving God. We have life experiences which, no matter how similar they may be, are by no means identical. All of us find unique intersections between opportunities for ministry and our own gifts – situations in which we can do what no other single person can do at that time. There are people each day of the week with whom we interact who need to know more about Christ's love. Our genuine interest in those people, combined with our own clear devotion to Christ and the church, can have significant impact.

CONCEPT: The support of other persons makes it much easier to take initiatives for church growth.

Significant growth often happens when a team of people in a parish begin supporting one another. Groups which meet once a week or once a month at the church or at a member's home to share in prayer and refreshments and then go visiting on behalf of the church can make a great difference. It would be good to study and discuss this book with a religious education class, a church board or committee, or a group of interested persons in the church.

It is not necessary to wait on that kind of discussion or joint work to begin having support. Start talking about the need for church growth and your personal response with just one other person right away who may be an active lay person, a staff member, or a spouse. "Getting started" inviting others to church and calling in homes is at least half the battle. The encouragement of others makes it easier to do this. Others do provide a sounding board for any experiences which prove frustrating.

Most people overestimate the amount of rejection they will have to endure when they begin to reach out to others and to encourage church involvement. When sincere, open approaches are made, people generally respond positively to us as individuals even if they reject the specific invitation. There are inevitably times when rejection is experienced. Whether the rejection is real or imagined, it still hurts. Having even one other person with whom to celebrate progress which has been made and with whom to share frustrations helps.

If you do nothing other than decide to invite someone new to church once a week or to make one call on a prospective member or an inactive member, by the end of the year you will see a significant difference as a result of your work. You can make an even greater difference if you involve others in your work. They'll support you, and they'll add to your efforts.

CONCEPT: Always remember that we are the agents through

whom God may choose to speak to the hearts and minds of others, but God is the one who changes the hearts and lives of people.

You and I can take too much responsibility on ourselves. We cannot "control" others. There is no action that is taken which will make another person believe in God or decide to be active in the church if that person is not ready for the experience. Salvation comes as a gift from God. Salvation does not come as the result of our sweat and toil.

We can witness to our own faith, sharing what Christ and the church have done in our lives and genuine concern for the other person. God is the one who must ultimately speak to the heart of that person, and the person then makes a personal decision about whether or not to be open to God's love.

God works in the lives of others through people and circumstances and situations which seem most unlikely. But God does not work under the limitations which we do. Remember that Moses felt his speech was not good enough to confront Pharaoh. Isaiah felt he was a person of unclean lips dwelling among a people of unclean lips. Jeremiah thought he was too young to carry God's message. But the Bible witnesses to the reality that God worked through all those people. God can and will work through us, not only through our strengths but also, at times, through our weaknesses. We should do our best, trusting the rest to God. We will not be disappointed in the results.

CONCEPT: Our work in church growth needs to be supported by a life of regular prayer, Bible study, and meditation.

Because our own strength and words and skills are inadequate, we need continuously to be in touch with the strength, love, and wisdom of God. Pray for those whom you are going to ask to attend church. Pray for those who have visited your church and on whom you are going to call. Pray for the persons who are inactive in your congregation. Pray for the work of other volunteers and church staff members.

Remember that Christ does love you and desires to work through you. As you increasingly open your life to Christ you will find ways of sharing the Good News which you never before thought possible. You will find it easier to forgive yourself when you fail to come across as you feel you should. You will find deeper thankfulness when your efforts make a difference in the church. And you will recognize more fully that in church growth as in all other things, although our human efforts are inadequate, the grace of God makes all things possible. For:

> *I can do all things in him who strengthens me.*
> Philippians 4:13

Do you think the work God gives us to do is never easy? Jesus says His yoke is easy, His burden is light. People sometimes refuse to do God's work just because it is easy. This is sometimes because they cannot believe that easy work is His work.... But however easy any work may be, it cannot be well done without taking thought about it. And such people, instead of taking thought about their work, generally take thought about the morrow, in which no work can be done any more than in yesterday. The Holy Present! Today is when we should do our work and give thanks for it.

George MacDonald

Overcoming Indifference

*I know your works: you are neither cold nor hot. Would that
you were cold or hot! So, because you are lukewarm, and
neither cold nor hot, I will spew you out of my mouth. For
you say, I am rich, I have prospered, and I need nothing; not
knowing that you are wretched, pitiable, poor, blind, and
naked. Therefore I counsel you to buy from me gold refined
by fire, that you may be rich, and white garments to clothe you
and to keep the shame of your nakedness from being seen,
and salve to anoint your eyes, that you may see.*

Revelation 3: 15-18

**CONCEPT: When people lead prosperous lives and at least
appear successful, they may miss the importance of sharing
Christ's love with others.**

When Christ warned that the rich have difficulty entering the
kingdom of Heaven, He had no hostility toward the wealthy. He
truthfully expressed what has happened in the lives of many of us in
North America. When one prospers financially, the protection of and
adding to the prosperity itself becomes an almost all-consuming task.

The more we have,
the more we want.

The more we have,
the more we fear the loss of what we have.
The more we have,
the more we envy those who have more.
The more we have
the greater the temptation to depend on our wealth rather
than on the love and mercy of God.
The more we have,
the greater become the anxieties and tensions within our lives.

Mother Teresa, whose life has been devoted to the lepers and the
poor of Calcutta, feels the greatest sympathy for those of us who are

affluent and says: "The spiritual poverty of the western world is much greater than the physical poverty of our people.... These people are not hungry in the physical sense but they are in another way. They know they need something more than money, yet they don't know what it is. What they are missing really is a living relationship with God" (Life in the Spirit, pp. 13-14).

How can we invest heart and soul in sharing the love of Jesus Christ with others when success by the standards of society becomes the idol which we serve? Gallup polls over the last several years have consistently show that most people in North America believe in God. Seven out of ten people claim local church membership. But no more than 12 percent can be described as "highly spiritually committed."

Most of us within the institutional church today would have gotten along well in the church of Laodicea to which such strong words come in the third chapter of Revelation. We are "lukewarm" in our faith and commitment. Because we have not learned to commit our lives fully to Christ we miss countless opportunities to do good for others and to make known the love of God.

Like those at Laodicea, we are actually not rich. We are rich by material standards. Even those of us who think of ourselves as lower middle class are absolutely wealthy beyond the imagination of one of the lepers served by Mother Teresa in Calcutta. But that is not true wealth. We are poor and naked because we have not learned what things are most important in life.

Why don't our churches grow? Why is average attendance at worship such a small percentage of the total church membership? Why are church finances always tight? While many answers can be given, perhaps the deepest, most painful, yet most insightful response is that our churches do not grow because we are trying to serve too many gods.

Many church growth manuals speak about curing indifference to the need for church growth and sharing the faith. Those manuals certainly are right. But the deeper indifference is not in nurturing church growth but in making God the center of our lives. Long term church growth depends on long term spiritual growth within our lives. People whose lives are centered on God reflect the light of Christ in their relationships with others.

CONCEPT: Church growth results in change, and many of us resist change in the local church.

Almost no one actually "opposes" church growth. Many of those whose attitudes are indeed a barrier to church growth would express absolute amazement if they were told that they are "barriers." Of course we want our churches to grow. Why wouldn't we? But much of what we gain from the local church comes through relationships and routines which become fixed over periods of time.

An adult Sunday school class has ten people in attendance every week. Six of the ten have been in the same class for fifteen years; the other four have been in the class for eight years. They know each other well with unspoken agreement on certain topics which are to be avoided and they gain immense personal support from being in this group. If two new people come to the class, comfortable routines change.

Sam Higgins ushers every Sunday morning. He has performed that service for his church for the past eleven years. He chooses the other ushers and has worked out the best way to handle most situations. A relatively new member of the church serving as an usher can upset Sam by suggesting that things should be done differently. More distressing is the suggestion that a far larger number of persons should be involved as ushers and that those persons should be rotated on a quarterly basis.

Sarah and Jim aren't "old time" church members. They've only been active in the church for two years. Their activity is centered on the senior high youth group. In fact, advising that group has become a major focus for Sarah and Jim's lives. A suggestion that the youth group might grow more effectively if there were two more adults helping them will not be well received necessarily. Sarah and Jim gain much of their own identity through leading the young people, and they are very reluctant to share that identity. The fear that they will verbalize is that new people won't be accepted well by the youth. There may be some truth in that. Their deepest fear is, however, that their own strong bonds with the young people will be weakened.

The trustees have great power at First Church. While the rules of the denomination limit people to six years on that group, the same basic people have rotated on and off for years. New members have been integrated into the group occasionally. But the suggestion by an enthusiastic pastor that several young adults and new members of the church should have the opportunity to serve as trustees will create considerable anxiety for those accustomed to routine.

Mrs. Swanson has sat in the same pew for the past thirty-three years. When he was alive, her husband sat next to her. Their children filled much of the pew while they were growing up. The presence of a new member who doesn't know that the pew "belongs" to Mrs. Swanson causes her great distress. She feels small and petty if she verbalizes that distress, but she can't help thinking the newcomer is insensitive and rude.

Many people maintain that small churches have the greatest difficulty growing because they are filled with so many situations and relationships as those described. It seems that such problems are greater in smaller churches than in medium-sized or larger ones. But the same dynamics are present in most situations.

Growth is virtually impossible without change. And change threatens those who gain much of their identity from things as they are.

In a book of almost prophetic insight, *Future Shock*, Alvin Toffler pointed out that the increasing pace of change in North American society was going to shake the foundations for many people who simply could not keep pace with the rate of change. Toffler maintains that in times of massive change people need "stability zones." Many persons see established churches as stability zones in an uncertain world. Even persons who in theory may agree with the importance of change and acknowledge that the change is positive nevertheless may feel resistive and resentful.

As we work for church growth, we need to recognize that persons who resist change may not oppose change in itself as much as the invasion of what, for them, are important stability zones. Our plans for church growth must take into consideration the genuine need for a sense of continuing community and stability of those who are already active n the church.

ARE YOU OPEN TO CHANGE? *Most of us like to think that we are. Think about your practices and habits in the church. Check as many of the following as apply:*

_____ I normally sit in the same place at each worship service.

_____ I have been on the same board or committee for more than two years.

_____ I have been a member of the same class or group for more than two years.

_____ I consider myself very much involved in major decisions that affect the life of the church.

_____ Some of my closest friends are people with whom I

am involved at church.

Think about how you would feel if the addition of new members to your parish changed one or more of the above.

CONCEPT: Concern about institutional survival and internal church problems can motivate greater concern for church growth, but our approach to nonmembers should be expressed in other ways than institutional anxiety.

The last chapter of this book contains a "Church Growth Quiz" and some alarming statistical facts about what has happened in the decline of many churches. Sharing that information with leaders in your church can do a great deal to get their attention.

In many situations, changes in attitude toward church growth have to begin with concern about institutional survival or internal problems. Members often get concerned because of observations like these:

• Consider how many of our member are over sixty-five years of age. Whose going to pay the bills as these members move away and pass away?

• Consider how many younger members have moved in the past three years. If we don't start replacing more of them, how will we ever get enough youth group advisors or teachers?

• The same people always have to do the work in this church. We let lots of folks get "burned out," and then they don't want any more involvement at all. We need some "new blood."

• Our church used to be able to afford its own pastor. Now we have trouble paying our "fair share" for the pastor employed by us and a neighboring church. I wish we could get enough members to have a full time pastor again.

• We had an enormous youth program years ago. Now we just have a handful of young people. We need some new, energetic young adults in this church to help us build a good youth program again.

• The average age in the women's society keeps going up. We should have meetings on more evenings and weekends, but most of our members are homemakers or retired. Coming out in the evening isn't pleasant for them. We'd be glad to change things if we could get some younger members though. The group is literally going to die off if it keeps going as it is now.

• It costs a fortune to heat this building in the winter. It seems as if a bigger percentage of our budget goes toward maintenance of the building rather than to expand our ministry. If we could just get more members and more income, things would improve.

• It used to be that we didn't get along well with the church down the street. We don't understand baptism and communion the same way. But we've been doing more together since their membership and ours started to decline. If we can't get more members, we may have to think about a merger with them. If we do that they'll take over because they have more people.

Some of the situations just described no doubt exist in your own church or in churches with which you are familiar. All of those situations initially can nurture church growth because they make active members more conscious that a church holds even on membership, grows, or dies. After a certain number of years of decline, even holding even on membership may mean that valued programs and facilities cannot be maintained.

Unfortunately, awareness of these realities and of the depressing statistical information from the national level does not necessarily result in church growth. Too often the resulting motivation for going after new members becomes one of institutional survival.

We may say: "Our church could benefit from the involvement of a young couple like you. We need a younger perspective. It's hard for people my age to know what teenagers in the church need." The couple hears: "This church wants us to take on their youth group. But they aren't going to want us telling them how to spend their money."

We may say: "Our church needs to take its responsibility to people who have gone through a divorce or experienced difficult times more seriously. It isn't our place to judge people for what has happened in the past. You're a talented person, and we'd like to have you be a part of St. Matthew's." The person hears: "You really don't approve of divorce or you wouldn't bring up judgment at all. You may not approve of me, but you're losing members and need my involvement. I have skills that the church would like to use."

We may say: "We could really use the skills of a person like you in the church. We have rooms in the religious education building that need renovation. You could give us guidance." The person hears: "I could paint a lot of rooms and build some things for you. But you aren't about to let me be on the trustees and really make decisions about the use of the church building."

We may say: "The support of the church has come from too few people for too long. We need new blood to help us decide new priorities and to get the support of the church up to what it should be." The couple hears: "The church budget is in trouble. They see us living in a nice home and driving a nice car and that we're both working. They think we're good for at least a couple of grand a year to the church."

Ironically, the couple probably would enjoy working with young people. The divorced woman almost certainly would enjoy using her skills in the church. The painter and builder would find genuine satisfaction in helping to improve the physical facilities. The couple would probably feel better about themselves and about the church if they were active and were making a significant financial contribution.

The problem in each instance is that those who are being approached hear not just the words which are said but the underlying anxiety about the future of the congregation. They fear they are being pursued not for themselves or out of concern for what the church can give them but for ways in which they can be used or manipulated by the church.

People have automatic "garbage detectors." When our real concern is institutional survival rather than a ministry of sharing Christ's love, prospective and inactive members will detect the root concern. The response to that concern then may be negative.

Concern about the church as an institution is a fine starting point to motivate people who have been apathetic too long or indifferent toward church growth. But we must move people quickly beyond the concern for survival to an understanding of our need to share Christ's love with others who need to receive and share that love.

CONCEPT: Most churches need an intentional effort at overcoming indifference and cultivating attitudes which help church growth.

You as an individual can start that process as you talk to others. Tell friends in the church of your concerns about church growth and about the attitudes which are conducive to church growth. If you are a lay person reading this book, share it with your pastor. If you are a pastor, share it with your key lay people.

Tell others why you feel church growth is important. Share with them some of the barriers that you see to church growth. Help them recognize the attitudes which are helpful.

Think about the persons who are most likely to be threatened by the changes which may be necessary for church growth. Make a special effort to reach out to those persons, to stimulate their concern about sharing Christ's love, and to enlist them as allies (rather than adversaries) in efforts at church growth.

When you cannot convince people to become allies and to be more open to change, then prayerfully keep yourself aware of the insecurities which block them from the attitudes you wish that they had. They are not intentionally thwarting you. They probably would like to see the church grow also. But their lives are surrounded by conflicting pressures from work, money, family, and so forth. They feel threatened by increasing change all around them and value the stability of the church. Their own need for that stability is so great that they just can't accept the need for change in order to permit growth.

Work at sharing perspectives in one to one visits, through sermons, through adult education classes, and through discussions in administrative boards and committees. Over a period of time, you'll find increasing numbers of people concerned about church growth and sharing the faith.

Remember as well that whatever you do that nurtures spiritual growth almost inevitably will help church growth. People whose lives are centered more fully on Christ find it easier to reach out to others and to tolerate or even encourage change for the good of others. Don't suggest to those who are indifferent to church growth that their indifference is a result of weak faith. That charge will threaten them and generate hostility. Simply work toward spiritual growth, knowing that many attitudinal changes will result.

CONCEPT: Work whenever possible by adding people and opportunities rather than by making unnecessary change in existing programs and opportunities.

Don't make change for the sake of change.

Don't needlessly threaten those who are insecure.

When you see that new members need to become part of boards and committees, try to add these persons in addition to those who are already on the boards and committees. This is almost always better than replacing persons already in those groups. Work to add more than one person at a time so that newer persons have support bases when they become part of a continuing group. Have faith that in time people can learn to work together more effectively.

Consider starting many new groups in the church for spiritual growth and study. Chapter thirteen provides more guidance on starting new groups. Adding a new group is often much easier than adding new or prospective members to an existing group. Have some new groups that are primarily for new members, but also integrate older and newer members in as many activities as possible for the overall harmony and well being of the church.

Settings for Overcoming Indifference and Cultivating Attitudes Which Lead to Church Growth:

Sermons and homilies
Church board and committee meetings
Religious education classes and groups
Social organizations in the church
Discussion in prayer and Bible study groups
Special study groups to discuss a book like Plain Talk About Church Growth
Visits with key leaders in their homes
Informal dinner parties or coffees to share concerns for the future of your church with key leaders
Clarifying your own ideas with your husband, wife, or a friend
Articles in the parish bulletin and newsletter
Letters of concern to church leaders

Attitudes Which Lead to Church Growth:

Concern for institutional survival of the local church, if that concern does not become an obsession which excludes more positive motivations
Genuine love for Christ and the church and a desire to share that love
Genuine interest in other persons as unique human beings and a desire to better know those persons
A positive view of the church and a willingness to share those positive characteristics with others
A willingness to reach out to others, a willingness even to risk embarrassment by asking others for their names; an understanding that others may sometimes forget who we are
An enjoyment of good conversation
A willingness to work; to go from house to house inviting other to become active in the church and sharing what the church has done in your life
A recognition that we alone cannot bring others to Christ or make the church grow; Christ changes the lives of others; we provide channels through whom Christ's love can flow

4

A Marketing Look at Your Church

I appeal to you, brethren, by the name of our Lord Jesus Christ, that all of you agree and that there be no dissensions among you, but that you be united in the same mind and the same judgment. For it has been reported to me by Chloe's people that there is quarreling among you, my brethren. . . . For consider your call, brethren; not many of you were wise according to worldly standards, not many were powerful, not many were of noble birth; but God chose what is foolish in the world to shame the wise, God chose what is weak in the world to shame the strong . . .

1 Corinthians 1: 10-11, 26-27

All churches have problems. Paul expresses genuine frustration with the church at Corinth for the dissensions which had arisen there. The Corinthian church had developed factions. Paul was so distressed that he was thankful not many of the Corinthians could say they were baptized in his name. Most of the divisions and tensions which frustrate us in local churches today also threatened the future of the early church. The church rode through the storms of that day, and we can be confident that the church will survive the storms of our own day. While the Church (with a capital C) is indeed the body of Christ and Christ is the head, we experience the church as a human institution with shortcomings and problems. Our own inability to change the congregation for the better at times angers or disappoints us. But the people of Paul's time also found themselves unable to accomplish what they wished. Paul reminds them rather pointedly that they were not chosen for their work in the church because they were wise or powerful. God has always been able to work through the weak as well as the strong and the foolish as well as the wise. Those are humbling words (especially if you were an original recipient of the letter to the Corinthian church!), but they are also encouraging words. We do not need to fear that we are unable to improve the church and carry out the ministry which Christ wishes. By his grace, Christ gives us the strength needed to do his work. This chapter suggests that you take a "marketing look" at your congregation. Facing some pointed questions now can put you in a better position to represent your church favorably to others.

CONCEPT: Know the strong points of your church, and be sure that members and prospective members are aware of them.

Sounds obvious? Not necessarily. Those who are most active in a local church sometimes understand better the weaknesses than the strengths of that church. That is understandable. We want to improve the church, so of course we try to understand areas of need. That does not mean active church members have no awareness of the church's strengths. It is just that they may take those strengths for granted. In their interactions with disgruntled church members or with prospective members, however, they may present the church in an unfavorable light unintentionally by not saying enough about the congregation's strengths.

Churches change. Someone may have joined your church ten years ago at a time when the youth program was weak and mission outreach was strong. In the last ten years, it is possible that the youth program has grown strong and the mission outreach weak. But if those who joined ten years ago do not have children active in the youth program, they may not be aware of the positive change in that area.

Work with other church leaders to identify all the strong points of your church. Don't let modesty get in the way! Let others know about those strong points. Be sure to ask some people who have joined in the last two or three years the main reasons for which they joined.

Consider making a brochure with a title like:

- **What I Like About St. Matthew's**
- **Why I Joined First Church**
- **Why I Think You'll Like Community Church**

Use representative statements from active members – includingsome who have been members for years and some who joined recently. Share this with prospective members but also share it with those who are already active.

CONCEPT: You also need a frank understanding of the shortcomings of your church, especially as those may appear to a prospective member. From that knowledge, you can find ways to make improvements and also learn more about the prospective members who are most likely to be interested in your congregation.

Again, be sure to ask persons who have recently joined about the negative factors as well as the positive ones. If you feel especially brave, you may learn a great deal by visiting with persons who considered joining your congregation and decided not to do so. Looking at faults can be a painful process, but we can learn a great deal. Don't automatically initiate programs to "remedy" every fault! Some energy may be better utilized expanding on the strong points of your church.

And weakness sometimes represents the other side of strength. If your church has a healthy, strong family life focus, your church may as a result be weaker in work with singles and couples who have no children. If your church has the plus (to some people) of church school classes and worship services going on at the same time (so adults can worship while children are in church school), the minus may be an adult education program that is weak (because so many people choose to be in worship rather than church school). While you may well be able to make improvements, remember that we are continually making choices in churches.

An understanding of faults and shortcomings can clarify the kinds of people to whom your congregation will be most attractive. That may help you narrow the focus of outreach. Some large downtown churches have found that they cannot compete successfully with more suburban churches for families with teenagers and small children. But those same churches may find that they can offer singles and couples with no children opportunities and a sense of belonging that are hard for these persons to experience in a "family church."

CONCEPT: What appears to be a weakness in your church program can sometimes be turned into a strength with a prospective member.

Inconsistent with what the rest of this chapter has said? Not necessarily. Consider a church in a suburban location that has difficulty involving many young singles in its program. If you are calling on a young single who is a prospective member, you don't want to make glowing statements about the opportunities available for a single person in your church. If the prospective member joins in part on the basis of those statements and then finds they were not true (or were "slight" exaggerations), then you'll end up with another resentful, inactive church member. It is better for your church and the Kingdom of God for that person to join another congregation.

But there is another way to approach that person. Consider saying something like this: "I'm afraid we don't have the number of programs for young singles which I wish were available. To be perfectly frank, we don't have a lot of young singles in the church. That obviously makes it difficult to develop the programs that we ought to have. I would, however, really like to see you become a member of First Church. You'll find that you can feel included in one of the adult classes and that people will be delighted to have you on a board or committee to help us respond better to the needs of other young people. If you are looking for an opportunity to interact with people representing a wide age range and for a place where your opinions will really be valued, I think you'd find First Church a great place to be."

If you can sincerely share that kind of statement you'll find many people who will respond positively to the opportunity. People don't always join a church for the great programs which are already there. Sometimes they join a church in part from a desire to feel needed and that their contributions are going to make a difference. In making this kind of approach, you have to walk a thin line. On the one hand, you should be genuinely interested in that person joining your congregation whether he or she does anything to help further the program life of your church or not. If you appear to want that person only for the work he or she might do, then you'll send up a red flag. On the other hand, you do want to help make the prospective member see that there are genuine opportunities to make a difference in your church.

The climate for "making a difference" will be much better if active members have a realistic view of the strengths and limitations of your church.

A MARKETING QUESTIONNAIRE FOR YOUR CHURCH

If your church employed a secular marketing consultant, that person would ask pointed questions to help you identify the strengths and weaknesses of your church from a marketing point of view. That consultant would finally recommend that you promote your church hardest to those groups and individuals who are most likely to be attracted by your strengths. He or she would also recommend that you do all you can to maximize strengths and minimize weaknesses. You may wish to have a group of people, including some relatively new additions to your church, complete this questionnaire and then discuss responses.

1. Will a visitor to your church have difficulty understanding anything about the order of worship or liturgy? If so, what?

2. What is the probability that a visitor to worship services in your church will receive a warm greeting on entering the church and the sanctuary? Will that greeting come from anyone in addition to greeters or ushers who have been formally designated for that purpose?

3. What age groups and social groups appear to dominate your membership from the perspective of someone visiting worship? If you have more than one service, does the answer to this question depend on the service attended?

4. How will the music of the service appeal to prospective members? Is it more likely to appeal to the young than the old? Is it more likely to appeal to those who like "old time" hymns and gospel music, to those who like folk music, or to those who especially enjoy classical music?

5. Would you describe your church as more "high church," more "low church," or something in the middle? "High church" would normally be a term associated with lots of printed liturgy and a relatively formal service. "Low church" would refer to very little printed liturgy and a relatively informal service.

6. How is the sermon or homily normally presented? Is the basic appeal to a highly educated person or to one who is not especially well educated? Would you describe most sermons as primarily Biblical, primarily building up the spiritual life, primarily confidence building, or primarily centered on social and global issues? If you would use more than one of those phrases, which would you use most heavily? Are your pastor's sermons well prepared?

7. How frequently is communion served in your church? In some denominations, this happens every Sunday; in some denominations, it may only happen a few times a year. How comfortable will a visitor from another denomination feel with your communion practice? If your communion is not an "open communion" (in which anyone may participate, whether a member or not), how is that interpreted to keep visitors from making embarrassing mistakes?

8. How attractive are the physical facilities for worship? For

fellowship times? For education and youth work? What do your physical facilities suggest about the priorities of your church? What improvements are very much needed?

9. How would you describe the parking and rest room facilities of your church? How easy is it to find your church's location, a parking spot, and a rest room? Could a person drive around for several minutes trying to find the building only to be uncertain where parking is permitted? Are the rest rooms found easily, and are they clean and in good condition?

10. How would you describe the strengths and weaknesses of your educational program? For what age levels do you do the best job? Do you have an adequate number of well-trained teachers and leaders? Do teachers make routine efforts to help visitors feel welcome? Do you have good follow up on visitors to your education programs?

11. How would you describe the strengths and weaknesses of your youth program? What kinds of young people are actively involved? What kinds of young people are not likely to want to share in your programs? Do youth in your church feel as if they are an important part of the church program? Do the active young people have strong bonds between them? Are those bonds so strong that a newcomer may have trouble feeling accepted?

12. Do you have short-term study groups and retreats available? These can be excellent ways to involve prospective members and new members. If these opportunities are not available, how difficult is it for people to be integrated into existing classes and groups?

13. How would you describe the quality of communication in your church? How much communication of special events comes from special letters, from worship service announcements, from the bulletin, from phone calls, from a newsletter? How quickly can a prospective member begin to feel that he or she has a good "feel" for the program of your church?

14. What kind of job does your church do in providing pastoral care to those who are in hospitals and nursing homes? For those with other special needs? How much of this is done by the pastor? By lay persons? To what extent do you hear reports of appreciation for the pastoral care which has been given? To what extent do you hear reports of neglect? Would you feel comfortable talking to

prospective members about the high level of pastoral care in your church?

15. How would you describe your church office? Does it suggest a well organized, efficient parish? Or does it suggest a staff (of one or more persons) who care deeply about people but who are not well organized? Does the office need to be more comfortably furnished to help visitors feel welcome and at ease?

16. What kinds of day care, nursery school, parochial school, and similar outreach educational services are offered by your church? What is the quality of these? To what extent are people in the community aware of what is offered?

17. Is your church adequately staffed with employed persons and volunteers? Or are the staff and volunteers continuously overworked? Are staff members accessible when lay persons need to visit with them about the church's program or about personal needs? Can you talk comfortably about the willingness of staff to help people with personal problems?

18. What does your church do in outreach to the poor and hungry of the world? Do you have a food pantry, emergency fund, or other form of local outreach to the poor? Do you participate in denominational or nondenominational programs to help the hungry? What kinds of missions outreach do you have to share the good news of Christ around the world? Will people who care deeply about outreach be convinced that your church cares and gives opportunities for service?

19. How broadly shared is leadership in your church? Do you have a good balance of young and old on committees and boards? Do you have persons who are relatively new members in key leadership positions as well as persons who have been active in the church for a long period of time? How do people in the church perceive leadership? Do most people feel it is broadly enough shared, or do some resent how decisions are made?

20. What age levels and family situations are most strongly represented in your church? Children? Teenagers? Young adult? Middle aged adults? Older adults? Families with children at home? Families with grown children? Single parents? Couples with no children? Retired persons? The handicapped? Persons of specific

ethnic background? How do these correspond to persons in your community?

21. Does your church have a history of dissension? Are there persons in your church who strongly dislike one another and make very little secret of it? Is there a danger that people will want a new member to "choose sides" in some continuing dispute? What kind of image of Christian love and unity does your church give?

22. Do many members have a particular image of your church? For example: a country church, a farmers' church, a teachers' church, a white collar church, a blue collar church, a family church, a church of the affluent, a church of social climbers, a bankers' church, and so forth. How correct or incorrect are those images? How do those images relate to the realities of your community and sources of prospective members? How widespread are those images? Are the images seen as primarily positive or primarily negative?

23. Do people in your church tend to talk readily about their personal faith? Or are people very uncomfortable talking about matters of personal faith? Do people talk readily about the good experiences they have had in the church? Or are they more likely to talk about what they find uncomfortable about the church?

24. What conveniences (or inconveniences) does your church offer for persons in certain life situations? How accessible is your building for someone in a wheelchair? How safe is your building for someone with vision problems? What arrangements have been made for those who have difficulty hearing, and how comfortable do people feel taking advantage of those arrangements? Are baby sitters provided during worship and church school? Are sitters provided during evening and weekday programs of the church? Is there a charge for that service? Do people have to make advance reservations for baby sitting or child care, or is it automatically available whenever there are activities at the church?

Now review the comments which you've collected and identify the key strengths and weaknesses of your congregation which should be considered in efforts at church growth.

Strengths:

1.

2.

3.

4.

5.

6.

7.
8.

9.

10.

Weaknesses:

1.

2.

3.

4.

5.

6.

7.

8.

9.

10.

What kind of person (or persons) are most likely to be attracted to

your church?

What kind of person (or persons) are least likely to be attracted to your church?

5

Where Are the Prospects?

*Then he said to his disciples,"The harvest is plentiful, but the
laborers are few; pray therefore the Lord of the harvest to send
out laborers into his harvest."*

Matthew 9:37

While the vast majority of people indicate a "religious preference"
in response to questions on national polls, far fewer are actually
members of an organized church. Depending on whose figures you
use, around ninety million Americans are not local parish members.
Of those who are members, a whopping percentage continue to be
relatively inactive–enough so that only one in eight Americans can
be called "highly spiritually committed." The words of Christ to the
disciples continue to be relevant in two ways.

First, the harvest truly is plentiful. According to the account in
Matthew's Gospel, Christ spoke of the plentiful harvest when he saw
great crowds, eager for the message and healing which he brought.
People in twentieth-century America continue to hunger for the
message of Christ and for his healing power in their lives.

Second, it is no easy task to reach out to people in ways that will
bring them into full involvement in the church–it is a lot of work,
and the laborers are few!

This chapter shows you several ways to find prospective members
in your own geographical area. While some of these approaches
obviously yield the greatest results in areas of high population growth,
most of them will produce prospective members regardless of your
location. But most of these approaches also involve a considerable
amount of work. There are no easy answers.

When we see our outreach as sharing the love of Christ rather than
simply building up the church as an institution, then that work can be
a pleasant, meaningful process.

It is still work. The prospective members who visit your worship
services constitute one of the most likely groups to join. Don't lose
them! Keep attendance records, and make certain that people are
visited within a few days of their first visit to your worship services.

As strange as it may seem, each Sunday morning tens of thousands of prospective members walk into local church worship services around the United States but do not end up becoming members of those churches. Why?

Sam and Betty Johnson have just moved to a southwestern city. On their third weekend in town, they decide it is time to find a church home. They were active members of a downtown Presbyterian church in their last community. They seek the same kind of church in this one. Sure enough, they find First Presbyterian located downtown. The church, in physical appearance, reminds them of the church in which they were active before.

They have trouble finding a parking place and are not sure which of the big doors to use in entering the church. There are big doors at what looks like a main entrance to the sanctuary, but no one else seems to enter by those doors. They go in a side entrance, and a pleasant appearing woman directs them to the sanctuary.

The worship service seems familiar to them, but they are surprised to find how young the senior pastor is. The senior pastor in their last church was in his early sixties; this one can't be much past forty. The service goes reasonably well, but they enter and leave without actually meeting anyone. They leave the church by the door where an associate pastor is shaking hands with people and introduce themselves to him as new residents in the community. He gives them a warm greeting and asks if they registered their attendance. They respond that they did, and he tells them he very much hopes they will be back the following week. They respond by saying they will.

On Thursday of that week, they receive a copy of the church's newsletter and a note signed by the senior pastor. The address label for the newsletter and the pastor's note both have their last name misspelled. They can understand that. Sam completed the registration and has atrocious handwriting.

They talk about going back the next week, but the week has been a busy one. They decide to sleep late that morning. Another week goes by and another week. Two months later, Sam and Betty still receive the church newsletter; but they have not returned to the church.

The church did many things right. Chapter twelve on worship will provide more specific suggestions on arrangements at worship services. Consider for the moment the things that happened over which the church had control:

• A clearer marked entrance to the church would have helped, but the absence of that was not a major obstacle.

- A woman was quick to direct them to the sanctuary.
- The order of service was sufficiently familiar that they felt all right about the service. Certainly there was nothing wrong in the fact that the senior pastor was younger than they expected.
- The associate who greeted them was careful to be sure they had registered their attendance and invited them to return the following week.
- The church efficiently got them on the newsletter list and continued sending the publication for two months.
- The church office prepared a note to them which was signed by the senior pastor. Handwriting on registration pads can be impossible to read. It is no one's fault that the name was misspelled.

So most of what happened was positive. What did the church do wrong? The misspelled name and the lack of a clearly marked entrance were not significant factors. The church failed because no clear plan was made to have a church representative visit with Sam and Betty at their home the following week.

Sam and Betty were prime prospective members. There was not time for the associate pastor to have a lengthy visit at the door. But a visit in their home that same week by a staff member or by a lay volunteer could have made an enormous difference. Certainly a visitor would have found out how their name should have been spelled. The same visitor would have discovered that they had been active in a Presbyterian church in their last community and would have learned something about their areas of interest in the church. Five minutes of conversation would have let the visitor know that Betty loved participation in the choir at their last church. A further follow up later that same week from a choir member would have been very well received by Betty. A response that quickly would have let both Sam and Betty know that First Church wanted them as members.

Sam and Betty do not feel alienated. They do not feel unhappy with First Church. But they feel indifferent. The longer they are in the community, the fuller their schedules become. Their name will probably come off the newsletter list when someone at the church decides it is time to weed out people who get the newsletter but don't belong or donate any money to the parish.

No two actions will do more to identify prospective members and turn them into active members than consistently:

1. Having worship service attendance registration and identifying visitors in that way.

2. Having a staff member or a volunteer make a call at the home of prospective members within a few days of the worship service.

This also is the "100 percent certain" way to know who among those who visit worship services are genuinely prospective members who should be cultivated further and those who came for other reasons (while on vacation or because a friend was baptized or . . .). This is also the certain way to obtain other information about the needs and interests of those who have visited so that there is opportunity to have other persons in the parish contact them.

Most Roman Catholic parishes are not accustomed to taking an attendance registration, but the process does not have to be a difficult one. Pads or cards provided in the pews and a short explanation from the liturgist can get the process started. Roman Catholic Churches can probably borrow some registration forms from nearby Protestant churches.

Protestant churches often have a registration of attendance but too often do not use that information effectively. Names and addresses of persons to be contacted should be prepared early in the week.

CONCEPT: Every parish has many different "ports of entry" for prospective members. Your parish needs to have a system to be certain that information gets shared.

Think about the number of different groups and organizations in your church. Unless your church is extremely small, you have:

- One or more choirs.
- Religious education classes.
- A youth group.
- A women's group.

You may also have a men's group, Bible study groups, additional musical groups, prayer groups, work groups, service groups, social groups, and a range of other opportunities. While many prospective members will "try out" your parish by attending worship services, others will begin their activity by coming to a choir rehearsal with a friend, attending a Bible study group, coming to a youth retreat or attending a women's group supper. Not everyone who visits a group in the church constitutes a prospective member, but many do.

Be certain that appropriate records are maintained so that the staff or a volunteer can make a follow up visit on anyone who shows an interest in your parish. The church office generally should keep centralized listing of visitors and prospective members. All groups in the parish should make a regular practice of sharing names and addresses of visitors with the office. There should be a regular system of follow-up on those persons. While such systems are especially important in medium sized and larger churches, they can be of considerable help even in relatively small churches. The fact that a church is small does not automatically keep visitors from "slipping through the cracks" if everyone assumes that someone else will follow through!

CONCEPT: A short survey of persons who visited your parish over a thirty to ninety day period of time can help you identify weaknesses in your approach to visitors as prospective members.

Each church faces unique issues depending on its location, theology, physical plant, membership characteristics, and other factors. Few things are as revealing as a carefully done survey of persons who have visited your church over a thirty to ninety day period of time. Call these persons by phone, or arrange personal visits with them – whether they have joined your church or not. Find out from those visits how they felt about your church; what made them feel good; what made them uncomfortable. When you help people understand that candid responses are very important to you, the comments offered will help you to see the strengths and weaknesses of your church as viewed by a "first timer" (or "second timer" or . . .).

QUESTIONS: After explaining your purpose in doing the survey, be sure to ask those who have visited in the last thirty to ninety days:

- Why did you visit our parish?
- What did you like best when you visited?
- Were there any events which displeased you when you visited? If so, what were they?
- How warmly greeted did you feel when you visited?
- If you plan to join our parish, what are your reasons for joining? If you don't plan to join our parish, what are the reasons for not doing so?

CONCEPT: Your own church records, especially of children's classes and youth groups, may provide the names of many prospective members.

As indicated in the discussion of the last concept most churches have many different "ports of entry" for prospective members. The fact that people are "lost" as prospective members at one point does not necessarily mean that they cannot be reached in the future.

When a visitor has actually joined another church, your church records should reflect that fact. You should not spend more time or energy on that person as a prospective member. When a visitor clearly is not a candidate for membership in your church, that person should not be on a prospective member list.

But don't throw out those names of visitors until you are certain whether or not a particular person may be a prospective member. There may be some people like Sam and Betty who visited, were not motivated enough to come back, but have not found another church home. The process of contacting people to clean up your records (and thus enable you to concentrate staff and volunteer energy where the most good can be accomplished) may also reveal some prospective members.

Looking at religious education and youth group records will often identify two categories of prospective members:

1. Mothers and fathers of children and young people who are attending or have attended classes or groups in your parish. These are persons concerned enough to see to the religious education of their children but who, themselves, have not become active in a parish.

2. Children and young people who have become inactive but who have not affiliated with another congregation. St. Paul's had a fourth grade Sunday school class with eighteen students three years ago. Those students are now seventh graders which is the traditional time of membership instruction in that church. The records now reflect fourteen students from that same group. Two of those fourteen were not in the church three years ago. That means that a total of six persons who were listed on the roster and who attended three years ago are no longer attending.

What happened to those six at St. Paul's? It's quite possible that some of them moved out of the community, or that their parents of some of them have changed to another local church. But it's also possible that some of them simply became inactive and were dropped from the rolls. Another approach to those children and their parents may bring a significant change in activity, especially given the fact that many parents feel it is important for their offspring to go through membership instruction. Compare old class rosters with new ones.

CONCEPT: The normal time of membership classes in your parish provides a good opportunity to check your records and be sure that invitations are extended to all young people who are prospective members.

The concept just discussed talks about why a careful review of your records may reveal some persons who became inactive in the religious education program of your parish but may be reactivated for membership instruction. You may also find that young people themselves can be a great help. Have them share names of friends who do not have any local church affiliation. Those persons should be viewed as prospective members, and it may be appropriate for a staff member or volunteer to call on those persons. If you develop enthusiasm and pride in the membership preparation process, young people will be willing to talk to their friends about the classes.

Some churches are reluctant to do this kind of outreach for fear of getting more members who will simply become inactive at a later time. Considerable justification exists for those fears. But the answer does not consist of not trying to involve them in membership preparation; the answer consists of development a program and follow up of such high quality that you cut down significantly on the number of persons who become inactive. (More about that in future chapters.)

CONCEPT: Find as many ways as possible to identify newcomers to your community, including a neighborhood shepherd system if feasible for your parish.

During the first six weeks in a new community, most people are far better possibilities as prospective members than they will be again (until they move to another community—when they'll be prospects for someone else but not for you!). The quicker an invitation to attend church can get to these persons, the more likely that they will become members. There are several ways to deal with this.

Some communities have newcomer services and are willing to share the names of new residents with churches in the community. This is an excellent opportunity if available.

If parish members understand the importance of outreach and develop enthusiasm for representing the church, they can do an excellent job noting newcomers in their neighborhood and reaching out to them. Members who feel uncomfortable giving an invitation to church attendance personally can still share names and addresses with the church office which can in turn have another volunteer or a staff member make a visit to that household.

Some churches have organized geographically based "shepherd" systems. Active individuals or couples in the parish assume responsibility as the shepherds of particular geographical areas. The shepherd has two basic responsibilities:

1. To keep aware of pastoral needs in that neighborhood group, to respond to those needs when comfortable doing so, and to share information with the church office.

2. To stay aware of newcomers to the neighborhood, to invite those persons to attend church, and to share that information with the church office (which in turn sees that it is shared with other appropriate persons and groups).

The shepherd system may not work as well in some urban congregations which draw members from an extremely broad geographical area but have very few concentrations of members. Shepherds in those situations can still make periodic phone calls or visits to attend to the needs of those who are currently members, but it may be more difficult to obtain as much information about newcomers. In small, medium sized, and suburban communities, shepherd systems can be extremely effective. Remember as well that you don't have to cover 100 percent of the community for prospective members. Whatever portion you do cover will be of help to you.

You can also gain considerably by seeing that member of your congregation who are likely to have contact with newcomers are provided with information about your parish. While many of them are in positions in which it would be inappropriate for them to make a "pitch" for your church or to share with the church names and addresses of prospective members, they can still respond when persons raise questions about church opportunities and can let others know that they feel good about their own church involvement. This list of persons could include real estate brokers, insurance agents, bank employees, personnel directors, and anyone else likely to come in contact with newcomers to the community.

CONCEPT: Canvasses and surveys of neighborhoods and communities can give you many valuable leads on members for your parish.

A house-to-house canvass or survey of your community or of the neighborhood or neighborhoods considered the major area for your church's ministry can be an enormous help. There are several ways to approach this task:

- Through a telephone survey.
- Through a direct mail survey.
- Through a door-to-door survey conducted by your church.
- Through a door-to-door survey conducted by your church in cooperation with others.

Many communities have available "directories" which give names, addresses, and phone numbers by street. These are put together by private firms and are primarily used for marketing work by various organizations in the community. Some churches buy these directories; most libraries will have them; and real estate agents generally will have them. You can use this information to help you with letters, phone calls, or visits.

You can also do direct mail surveys to persons by address or box number rather than name. Check with your post office for details on that kind of mailing. A door-to-door canvass does not require any prior information about names.

The survey should be simple in focus:

- Explain that the purpose is to find out more about the community, the religious affiliations of people in the community, and the needs of persons in the community.
- Get current names, addresses, and phone numbers.
- Find out what "religious affiliation" people have and also whether or not they belong to a local church. Remember that more people will give a religious affiliation than actually belong to a local congregation.
- If you have a list of possible programs, ask persons to give you a response to that list. Which programs do they think would be beneficial to them personally? Which do they think would be beneficial to others in the community?
- If persons do not have membership in a church and appear at least moderately interested in the survey, you should be prepared to give them information about your church. But don't do a hard sell at the time of the survey. Simply giving them (or mailing them if you do a mail survey or phone survey) a brochure of information about your parish is an adequate first step.

Respect the rights of people who do not want to answer questions. When people say that they are members of another congregation and involved there, affirm that involvement. Don't try to "take" members from another church–there are plenty of good prospects without trying to raid another congregation!

Preparation for summer programs or fall programs gives an excellent opportunity for such surveys. You can find out persons who might want to share in summer Bible school classes, retreats, or camps. You can also identify persons interested in special fall opportunities.

Chapter eleven talks more about direct mail approaches to member recruitment.

CONCEPT: Television, newspaper, and radio ads can help the image of your church and give good service to others; but these approaches will not necessarily bring large numbers of members to your church.

While television, newspaper, and radio approaches can help any church, they are not necessarily the best way to reach prospective members. If well done, they can create a positive image for your congregation. They can also provide a valuable service to persons who are unable to attend worship services.

But a more personal invitation is generally needed to motivate people to visit your church. Television, newspaper, and radio ads may provide some added motivation for someone who already has interest or already feels pulled toward the church. These media, however, are best utilized as additions to other forms of outreach which are more "one to one" in nature. Chapter ten talks more about the use of these media.

CONCEPT: A good church computer system can help your church keep track of visitors and prospective members. It can also make the surveying process much easier for you to do.

No computer itself will ever add a single person to your parish membership. A computer can, however, make it far easier for you to keep track of visitor, prospective members, and survey respondents.

- The best systems make it easy for you to change the status of someone from visitor to prospective member to member. Then information only has to be entered one time.

- The best systems also make it possible for you to continue adding information as you learn more about the individual or household. It should be possible for that same information to be recalled, so that you can get lists by age, marital status, talents, interests, and so forth.
- The system should also make it possible for you to use a word processing program in conjunction with information on visitors and prospective members to prepare individually typed letters and envelopes without the work required to do each manually.
- Attendance records can be much easier to maintain on a computer system, and it can also be much easier to get reports of changes in attendance patterns which help identify visitors who are indeed prospective members (and active members who are in danger of becoming inactive!).
- Some church management software actually helps you construct surveys and record the data from them.

The larger your parish, the more you can gain from a good computer system. Be certain to buy software which can genuinely help you in outreach and not just keep track of parish finances. While your church certainly can make a good case for a computer system to keep better track of parish finances, you should be able to get software that will help you with outreach as well.

CONCEPT: Helping as many members as possible have a good understanding of the importance of outreach and how to go about it can be of great value.

Many people in the congregation would like to help your church grow and would like to better share the good news of Jesus Christ. But people often are not comfortable talking with others about their faith or inviting them to church. The more background you can provide, the better. Three specific suggestions:

1. Provide literature on your church which active members can share with friends and neighbors who may be prospective members. This makes it easier for them to initiate discussions and gives a specific purpose for making a contact. This should include not only literature about the overall church program and an invitation to attend but should also include special fliers about retreats, short term

classes, and other events which could be "ports of entry" or "getting started points" for people.

2. Involve members in study of a book like this one so that they have a good understanding of the importance of outreach and of the amount of difference which they can make.

3. Periodically remind people from the pulpit, in the newsletter, in classes, and in boards and committees of the need to be alert for prospective members and to let others know about the opportunities of your parish.

CONCEPT: Evangelism crusades and revival meetings can be important sources of prospective members.

Many churches which are growing rapidly do obtain new members through crusades and revivals. The crusade or revival may be sponsored by an individual church or may be conducted in cooperation with several churches. The words crusade and revival are often used interchangeably. Both terms refer to a special preaching event or series of preaching events to which the public is invited. The events may be held in the church, in a larger community facility, or in an outdoor tent or arena.

The most common distinction between a crusade and a revival is in the extent of outreach involved. Revivals are often held primarily for the spiritual renewal of congregation members but with some publicity to the surrounding community and with church members encouraged to invite friends and neighbors. A crusade is generally a much more intensive outreach to the community with great publicity and often sustematic calls or visits to persons in the community.

These events generally rely on the use of a preacher from outside the immediate geographical area. Sometimes these preachers are affiliated with organization which give considerable guidance to the overall preparation and organization of the event. In other instances, the speaker leaves all the organizational details to the local congregation(s). The choice of a speaker and organization is absolutely critical to the success of such an event. Before contracting with a speaker or organization:

1. Be certain you understand the theological orientation of the speaker. You need someone whose beliefs and theological vocabulary are compatible with your denomination and congregation.

2. Use a speaker who has been involved with other successful crusades or revivals. It is always good to make telephone contact with other churches who have worked with the speaker or organization.

3. Be certain financial terms are made very clear in advance. It is usually best to have those in writing. Practices vary widely. Some speakers come for free will offerings. While that kind of arrangement is tempting to a church since it involves no financial risk, remember that the speaker will often be the one making the plea for the offering. How that is done will reflect on your congregation. Others may charge a set fee plus expenses which the sponsoring church or churches must promise to pay, but any donations re eived in excess of that amount are retained locally.

4. Working with an organization rather than an individual speaker often brings the benefit of additional help in organizing the crusade or revival and planning for follow-up afterwards.

The Billy Graham Evangelistic Association continues to conduct the most campaigns of which I am aware. In addition to the major urban campaigns which feature Billy Graham as speaker, the organization conducts crusades in smaller cities utilizing associate evangelists who are also outstanding speakers. Even if your plans are much less ambitious in scope, the Graham organization is a good source of guidance. Their crusades are conducted according to very high ethical standards. Finances are well accounted for and raised without manipulation. The membership preferences of persons who make new commitments at the crusade are respected, and participating churches are not permitted to proselytize from one another.

The advantage of a large community-wide campaign which involves many churches is that the combined impact is much more likely to reach the nonchurched than smaller efforts by individual churches. Successful campaigns, however, are a great deal of work. The planning and organizational stages must begin many months in advance if the event is to be successful. A church's involvement in such a campaign will become a major program priority for the year, and that commitment should not be lightly made.

Local church sponsored crusades and revivals can also have significant impact. The more effort made to reach nonmembers, the more beneficial the event from the perspective of church growth. Many revival meetings provide needed spiritual uplift ocongregation members but really do little to gain new commitments to Christ and members for the church. If you are contemplating a crusade or revival, this checklist may be helpful to you in planning:

_____ Determine what your goals are for the event. Do you primarily want a renewal event for your own congregation, or do you want to reach nonmenbers? The decision will influence the speaker or organization you choose to work with and the kind of planning you do for the event.

_____ Choose dates which will be in as little conflict as possible with other church and community events.

_____ Form a planning or coordinating committee which includes persons from Christian education and youth work. It may be possible to have some special educational and youth events in conjunciton with the crusade or revival.

_____ Decide how best to approach newspapers and other media for publicity. If your speaker is well known or has impressive credentials, arrange interviews prior to the event as well as devotional spots on radio and television. Your success at getting your speaker on television will depend on the prominence of the speaker and on the willingness of the church to buy time.

_____ Have youth and children's groups and classes distribute posters and fliers about the event.

_____ Recruit and train telephone calling or home visiting teams to contact people in the community.

_____ Have the telephone teams or home visiting teams contact households in neighborhoods where you have high concentrations of members. A city director from your library or a real estate agent can help identify names and phone numbers by street.

_____ Have "minute speakers" at morning worship to build enthusiasm and to encourage memebers to invite friends and neighbors to the event. Give members fliers or brochures which they can give to others.

_____ If the crusade or revival is structured so that people are invited to make a new commitment to Christ, you need to have volunteers trained as spiritual counselors so they can visit and pray with those new commitments immediately. Have devotional literature and Bibles available to give to persons making new commitments.

_____ Develop a plan for follow-up after the event with persons who made new commitments to Christ. People are often swept up in the spiritual warmth of such events and make commitments which lose meaning when the event is over. Your church needs continued contact with these persons. They should be involved in existing or new church groups, directed in study, and helped to become responsible church members. The new commitment to Christ made at a revival or crusade is not the same as a commitment to join Christ's body, the church. It will only lead to a commitment to the church as those persons receive direction and help. If they don't become part of your church or another Christian community, it's very possible that they will not continue in the Christian way. It's virtually impossible to be a Christian in isolation.

_____ Develop a plan for follow-up on prospective members whose names were gained from neighborhood canvasses or who attended the event but without making a commitment to Christ. The fact that people did not attend the event doesn't mean that they aren't prospective members. Crusades and revivals have appeal to only a limited number of people. There are many who will be others who will attend and perhaps be deeply moved but not comfortable making a public profession of faith at the time of the crusade or revival. Finding these persons through the phone calls, neighborhood contacts, and general publicity is one of the major benefits of a crusade or revival.

Some people reading this book no doubt have little interest in a revival or crusade. Those approaches are not comfortable to persons of some religious traditions. Remember, however, that the concept presented here is one of crusades or revivals as special events with a focus on reaching nonmembers. Don't let the "crusade" or "revival" terminology block you from creative thinking about special events which could be attrative to nonmembers and can lead them into commitments to Christ. Themes like "Spiritual Life Emphasis" and "Growing Closer to God" can combine meaningful worship services with small group study and other creative approaches.

6

WHY PLANS OFTEN FAIL

An intelligent person aims at wise action, but a fool starts off in many directions.
Proverbs 17:24

People may plan all kinds of things, but the Lord's will is going to be done.
Proverbs 19:21

You can get horses ready for battle, but it is the Lord who gives victory.
Proverbs 12:31

St. Paul's Parish Council passed a unanimous resolution: they would seek a 10 percent increase in their parish school enrollment and in attendance at worship services in the year ahead.

Bradley Avenue's Commission on Evangelism established a goal of an 8 percent increase in membership for the coming year.

A national meeting for a major Protestant denomination endorsed with enthusiasm a program for 10 percent growth a year for the next four years.

But one year later, St. Paul's had only a 2 percent increase in parish school enrollment and suffered a 4 percent decline in average worship attendance. Bradley Avenue's membership dipped 1.5 percent. The Protestant denomination's rate of decline slowed over the previous year, but the drop was still 1.4 percent.

Whole forests have been sacrificed to print all the materials on parish growth over the last decade. Millions of dollars have been spent in people attending church growth conferences and institutes. Some churches have grown. Some have declined. But three out of ten people still aren't members of a local congregation (even though some of them claim a religious affiliation or identification), and only one out of eight Americans can be called highly spiritually committed by any reasonable definition. Our plans and ideas often fall short.

Let me summarize briefly some of the major points which I've tried to make thus far. You can help your parish grow by:

• Recognizing that you as an individual can make a difference and doing your own part to reach out to others and to influence attitudes and programs in your church.

• Helping change attitudes of parish members into ones more open to prospective members, more willing to reach out to others, and more willing to put time and energy into church growth.

• Building support through study with others of books like this one and sharing both in developing strategies and in doing the work needed for parish growth.

• Taking a prayerful approach to your work for the church, recognizing that God works through us to reach others – we may impede God's work in the hearts of others, but we cannot replace God's work.

The thrust of this book is practical and positive. There is benefit however, in pausing for a few pages to consider some of the reasons that so many presumably well laid plans and lofty goals haven't made a difference in many churches.

CONCEPT: Planning for growth at the national or regional denominational level just doesn't translate into specific results at the local church level.

Go through the minutes of national and regional meetings of most major denominations. You'll find a wide assortment of approved goals for church expansion and endorsed materials for parish evangelism. You'll also find that the actual growth and decline of that particular denomination seems to have little resemblance to those goals and materials.

The plain truth is that it's hard for a denomination to have impact on employed staff at the local church level and almost impossible to have impact on the average person sitting in the pew on Sunday morning. Many of the materials produced by the national and regional levels of major denominations have been of very high quality and have unquestionably helped many congregations. But when one looks at figures on a regional or national basis, that impact often doesn't match up to the impact of demographics and social trends in the country as a whole.

It's difficult for the national or regional level to take initiatives that make a great difference in local church programming precisely because the most effective local church programming originates at the congregational level. That's not an argument against the national and regional plans and work, and the materials may make a big difference in specific congregations. But we need to realistically consider the limitations of any plans at levels beyond the local church.

None of this means that national and regional levels can't do things to help church growth. There are some very specific actions that are best done at levels beyond the local church:

• Plans for new churches need to come from a regional or national level. While it's true that some local churches successfully begin new congregations without regional or national support those instances are the exception rather than the rule. It takes the regional or national level to develop overall strategies that take into consideration where people are moving and the best locations for new churches. Funding, staffing, and other resources needed for the start of a new church can best come from a national or regional level. It's also important that whatever "subsidies" are provided be large enough to let the new church get off to a good star but not so large that the new church takes too long to become independent.

• Regional and national levels can impact seminary training and continuing education for church professionals. Offering the appropriate emphases in these educational settings can give church professionals skills that will help them in their parishes.

• The regional and national level may be able to produce some helpful materials which can be used by the local church which is wanting to grow.

> CONCEPT: Local planning and goals for XX percent increase in membership or attendance will have no impact unless accompanied (1) by concrete plans for finding and following up on new members and inactive members and (2) by the commitment of active members to outreach in Christ's name.

Enthusiasm and commitment for church growth has to move from leaders in the church to other church members, and plans must be thorough and not partial. Many churches have an annual planning meeting or retreat for key leaders and take time to "dream." That dreaming almost always includes substantial growth in average attendance and in membership. Then the planning time comes to an end, and people are again caught up in the whirlwind of daily life – with pressures from continuing programs of the church, from secular employment, and from the family. The dreams and plans so boldly made become lost in the pace of life.

As a local church pastor, I would prefer the personal commitment to outreach and willingness to work of six church members to any resolution for growth endorsed by the top fifty church leaders. Plans shift and change. Commitment to outreach and willingness to work can be translated into warmth expressed to prospective members, phone calls made, letters written, and doors knocked on in the name of the church and Christ.

That's why the second chapter of this book carries the title "Church Growth Begins With You and Me." Obviously the broader that circle of commitment grows, the greater the change and growth made possible in your church. But you and others like you can make more difference than all the plans in the world.

Which is not an argument against planning. In fact the problem with goals and plans often comes in the plans not being sufficiently detailed or thorough. Some churches, for example, have experimented with television and radio programs and advertising to help draw more people to the church. Some of those efforts have worked. But that won't make people continue attending the church or decide to join the church. A $20,000 advertising program not supported by quick follow up on visitors and careful assimilation of people into the congregation will be money that was better donated to world hunger.

This book intentionally has sections related to a diverse range of approaches and local church program areas. There's good reason for that. You can't do everything; you do need to "pick and choose." But more than that, church growth generally happens when a local church starts doing things that work for church growth across its total program. Having the pastor and volunteers making lots of calls only to have worship and educational experiences that turn off visitors is a sad situation. The calls that are made can still make a great difference, but the calls will make so much more difference if there is sensitivity to outreach across the life of the church.

CONCEPT: Sensitivity to life's serendipities and to the Holy Spirit's actions may be as important as the formal plans that we make.

Many plans for church growth go astray for the same reasons as other plans in the church. Other things happen which take priority, or things just don't work out the way they were anticipated. In fact, rigid planning can end up producing the wrong plan.

My wife and I were looking forward to a leisurely supper for just the two of us at a favorite restaurant. Thirty minutes before we planned to leave, good friends that we hadn't seen for three years stopped by our home. They would have called, but they had forgotten that they were driving so close to our new location until they saw the interstate highway exit. We ended up having a bucket of Kentucky Fried Chicken. Then we rearranged our plans for the next evening to have the leisurely supper for just the two of us.

We kept a living room chair for years that didn't fit with the rest of our furniture. We had a cranky old tabby cat who loved the chair. She increasingly had trouble getting around the house, and she'd flop in that chair for hours at a time. The chair had cat hair so deeply embedded that no cleaning process would get it all out and the chair actually began to smell like the cat. Though we often planned to replace it, we weren't able to bring ourselves to do it until the cat died.

That's how all of our lives go. We alter plans because of unexpected events and overriding emotional reasons. Not all these factors represent positive serendipities or the work of the Holy Spirit. But many of them are valid reasons for adjusting what we'd intended to do or what we still want to do.

While many of the factors which thwart our plans in the local church seem like anything but positive serendipities, over the course of a year we are given many opportunities to reach out in the name of Christ. Consider for example:

• Pastor Watson was in a hurry to complete his hospital calls. One of his church members introduced him to her hospital roommate who was dying of cancer and not connected with a local church. The pastor's schedule was changed by the extra forty-five minutes he spent talking with the terminal patient.

He didn't have any second thoughts about the decision, and he certainly expected no particular benefit to come to himself or his church because of the visit. In the process of visiting her additional times in the hospital, he got acquainted with her son and his family. Two months later, he conducted her funeral. Four months later, because of his continued follow up, her son, his wife, and their three children became active members of his church.

• A new group for divorced persons started having their organizational meetings in a conference room at the library. They found in time that child care was expensive for several group members and decided they needed a meeting place where they could have room for child care and share the expense. They approached the Adams Street Church. Only one person in the group actually belonged to that church, and he hadn't been active for years. The pastor and the trustees understandably recognized that there would be some increased work and liability involved in letting the group meet there. But they decided it was the right thing to do. Over the next two years, the pastor became an informal advisor to the group. Four group members ended up joining that church; and three others resumed activity in other churches, giving much of the credit for their decisions to the warmth of the church that hosted them and that pastor's reflection of Christ's love.

• The students of a suburban high school grew increasingly angry about school policies which they took to be unfair and dictatorial. Some concerned students wanted to have a meeting off the school campus to talk about their grievances. Three of them contacted a young pastor in their community and asked for permission to meet in his church. He had considerable anxiety about what a meeting like that might be like and about how church members would react. But he couldn't make himself say no and recognized that they were going to meet regardless. He asked permission to come and requested that the meeting also be open to school administration and faculty. The church would give a neutral setting, and the pastor would insure that the primary purpose was to hear the student concerns. Those conditions were accepted, and two hundred students came to the meeting.

The meeting didn't resolve the problems for the students, and some faculty members who belonged to the church were initially angry about the meeting happening there. But the pastor handled responses with a kindness and sincerity that made it hard for people to stay mad at him even if they disagreed with what he had done. And over a period of a year, the consistency of concern for youth – and a willingness to risk on their behalf – earned that pastor and that church respect which brought many young people into youth group activity, then into commitment to Christ, and finally to church membership.

Notice the similarities in all the situations just described:

1. The "opportunity" was at first an inconvenience.

2. The decision made in each instance was the "right" thing to do, but there was no apparent evidence that the decision would do anything to help church membership.

3. The resulting membership gain came as a serendipity or as Spirit. There's no guarantee that similar actions in other situations will necessarily result in anyone joining the church. Trying to manipulate

such situations to cause people to join the church out of obligation would never work.

4. The pastor in each instance did attempt the kind of outreach which made it more likely that the church's concern for people would be felt by the persons involved. Lay persons can have such impact as well.

Concern about people and openness to the opportunities that come, no matter how inconvenient they may be or how much they may harm our previous plans, may provide unique possibilities as the Holy Spirit works among us, doing what we ourselves could not do.

CONCEPT: Church staff members and volunteers who have regular times of prayer and Bible study are the most likely to remain open to opportunities for outreach and ministry.

Prayer and Bible study center our lives on what's really important more than perhaps any other practice. Protecting time each day and each week to reflect on God's will for our lives helps our values and priorities increasingly reflect openness to Christ.

The opening quote from Proverbs is right. We may get "the horses ready for battle," but victory comes from God. Our plans and values must be as consistent as possible with God's, or any victories we gain will be hollow.

While we are properly concerned about the visible impact of our efforts in terms of church membership, attendance, and finances, by God's grace, there may be further impact which we do not see. A Sunday school teacher may have a positive impact on a child which will change the course of that child's life, and the teacher may never know that he or she had that great an impact. A church that receives strong criticism and even loses members for harboring refugees may make such an impressive witness to the secular world that some persons in other communities will be more open to the Gospel than in the past.

You and I can only measure part of our results. Only God's judgment is ultimate. We do our best work when we root our lives as firmly as possible in openness to God. The church will not grow in numbers or spirit unless we take our own spiritual growth seriously.

KNOCKING ON DOORS

Nothing Else Works As Well

And when Jesus came to the place, he looked up and said to him, "Zacchaeus, make haste and come down; for I must stay at your house today."
                                              Luke 19:5

While Christ's message and power drew Zacchaeus and others to him, Christ had no hesitation in reaching out to others. In fact he spent enough time in the homes of people like Zacchaeus that he was criticized for doing so!

The rapid spread of the early church came because Paul and others took the Gospel message to people. The apostles and disciples traveled extensively to reach others with the good news of Jesus Christ.

In our own time, there is simply no substitute for visiting people in their homes if we want their involvement in the church. Nothing else brings as great a return for the time and energy expended. And most of the suggestions in this book will not yield strong results unless supported by a program of frequent visits to homes.

CONCEPT: When people visit worship services or educational activities in your parish, a staff member or a lay volunteer should respond with a visit to that person's home within a few days.

Various studies consistently show that people respond with great warmth to a call shortly after their visit to worship services or educational activities. One Disciples of Christ study showed that 85 percent of worship visitors who received a home visit from a lay member within thirty-six hours of the church service returned the following Sunday. Percentages and quickness of response vary with the particular study, but you can normally expect that between 50 percent and 75 percent of those who visit your church on a Sunday for the first time will return for a second visit if they receive a visit from you within five days. Five days represents the longest period of time you should let go by without a visit at that person's home. Why?

1. The personal visit stands as a concrete expression of the church's

genuine interest in that person or family.

2. Some anxiety always accompanies a visit to a new church and a new group of people. Personal contact with someone from that church puts to rest much of that anxiety.

3. The call may well reveal interests and needs of the visitor to which the church can respond. These could include youth programs for a teenager, choir for an adult, and day care for preschool children. The visitor to the prospective member's home can share information about those programs and can also ask representatives of other church groups to respond with additional information and an invitation for participation.

4. There may be uncertainty about something that happened in worship or other questions which stand as possible barriers to the involvement of the prospective member. These can often be resolved in a short visit.

As a general rule, people worry too much about making the first call a lengthy one. In actual fact the first visit on a prospective member who has attended worship or an educational activity may often only need to be ten or fifteen minutes in length. That's generally enough time to extend a warm welcome to that person or family, provide some additional information about the church, and find out more of that person or family's background and interest in the church. The call does not need to be made by appointment. If no one is there, a card can be left and a return call made. If household members are busy, a short two or three minute visit at the door can be adequate and a return call scheduled if that seems appropriate.

The first contact can be by a lay person or a staff member. No research to this point shows that the identity of the initial caller makes a difference; the main benefit derives from a call being made promptly! There is evidence supporting the fact that people are more likely to join a church if interest has been shown by both lay persons and staff members. This suggests that while one person may want to assume the major responsibility for the cultivation of a given prospective member, contacts with the prospect over a period of time need to come from parish volunteers and staff.

Lay volunteers generally find the process of calling on prospective members easier when:

- There is a support base through a club, prayer group,

committee, or commission for those doing calling.
  • Some training has been provided to help people feel
comfortable making the call.
  • Literature about the church has been provided so that the caller
has something to which he or she can refer and   which
can be left with the prospective member.

CONCEPT: When doing "cold calling" on potential prospective
members, expect that several contacts will be needed before
someone decides to become a church member.

Calls to persons who have already expressed an interest in the
church by attending worship or another parish event are relatively
easy to make. The prospective member has already reached toward
the church; the church now responds. But the outreach program for
most parishes needs to include some visits to persons who have not
made that kind of expression of interest in the church.

These may be called "cold calls," because the purpose of the call is
to determine whether or not the person or persons in the household
may be prospective members. If there is no membership with
another local church and there is openness to the contact then future
calls will be easier to make.

If you are doing a neighborhood canvass to see which persons are
not actively involved in a church and to leave information about your
parish, then the calling may be most comfortably done in teams of
two. Each person gives support to the other. Remember, however,
that the chief value of pairing for such calls is in making the calling
process itself easier. If a person feels comfortable making such calls
on his or her own, FORGE AHEAD!

If you visit someone who has not attended activities at your parish
and whom you are meeting for the first time, don't expect the first
visit to make the difference. People who canvass neighborhoods in the
process of starting brand new congregations find that six to ten calls
are sometimes needed before enough relationship is established for
the person visited to agree to try the church.

There are some good reasons for this. Most people who choose a
particular church still do so because they have a relationship with a
friend, neighbor, or acquaintance who is active in that church. When
you are doing genuinely "cold calling," you don't know that
person – and that person doesn't know you. It takes time to build a
relationship. If you have the patience to continue visiting over a
period of time, consistently showing your interest but avoiding an
appearance of "pushiness," you will develop a relationship with that

person who is then far more likely to respond.

CONCEPT: Hospital calling and follow up calls after dismissal from the hospital can bring many people into parish membership.

Most churches have programs to provide support and care to those members who are hospitalized. Persons who are in the hospital, whether for surgery, a physical examination, the birth of a child, minor illness, major illness, or psychiatric needs, are almost always more concerned about religious questions and more appreciative of contact from the church than at other times.

If the hospital or hospitals which members of your parish use do not have a system which lets patients register their religious affiliation, work with hospital administrators to establish such a system. Without that, you will miss many members and potential members who are hospitalized. Also enlist the aid of your congregation through the bulletin, newsletter, and pulpit announcements in letting the church office know about persons who are ill.

Those who have done much hospital calling are well aware that many people who have been inactive for years will still indicate their church membership when they enter the hospital. There are also many persons who do not belong to a local church who will nevertheless indicate a religious affiliation such as "Methodist," "Baptist," or "Roman Catholic" when admitted to the hospital. Both of these categories of people should receive calls from your church. Your expression of concern at this critical time in that person's life may make an immense difference for that individual and for your parish.

[If you do hospital calling in such a major urban area that the list of persons who consider themselves"affiliated" with your denomination but who are not members of your parish is too large, work out a system with other local churches to "share" the responsibility of calling on these persons.]

The problem with our efforts at outreach through hospital calls generally comes in our failure to follow up when the person has been dismissed from the hospital. You should establish a clear parish program that provides for at least one visit to the home for anyone who has been hospitalized for anything other than the most minor conditions (and if that person has been inactive or is not a member, then you may still want to make the call). The follow up calls shows the continuity of the church's concern and may also provide opportunity to talk about involvement in the church. The follow up call can also be important for active members of your parish because the anxiety connected with a stay in the hospital doesn't completely disappear with dismissal from the institution. Warmth an concern expressed at these times can make a critical difference in the lives of those we serve in Christ's name.

CONCEPT: Cards and literature help!

Any person making calls at institutions or homes in the name of your parish should be provided with cards and literature that can be left. The card doesn't have to be particularly elaborate; it can simply provide the church's name and address with a place for the caller to write his or her name and phone. But the card can make a difference:

• The person being visited will find it easier to remember the name of the caller if a card is provided.
• The presence of the card generally serves as a reminder of the church's interest. Such cards often end up on the refrigerator door – which is a prime location in most households!
• If no one is home when the call is attempted, a card should always be left. This way the person or persons at least know of the church's interest. The same is true when hospital calls are made and the patient is not in the room at the time of the call.

Literature can serve similar purposes. Give special consideration to sheets or pamphlets which provide information about the major organizations and services in your church. For visits to hospitals and nursing homes, inspirational booklets can have special meaning. The literature also helps persons who are reluctant to make these calls. Leaving the literature provides a purpose for the call and a potential focus of discussion.

While cards and literature do not have to be elaborate, they should be attractive and carefully written. Many denominations provide literature about the church and for hospital calls which can be used with your church's name and address or modified in ways more appropriate for your parish.

CONCEPT: The weeks immediately preceding and following Easter and Christmas are ideal times for calls!

Even in our highly secular society, Easter and Christmas stand as powerful reminders of the importance of religious activity. Many people who have been inactive for months will return to church in celebration of those days. Pastors and lay persons are well aware of the "Twice a Year Christians" who only turn out on those occasions.

But one of the best ways to bring them back on a regular basis is to call during the Easter and Christmas seasons. Some churches have special calling programs at the start of those seasons; some have the programs following Easter and Christmas; some choose to do heavy calling both before and after those special days.

CONCEPT: All parishes need substantial numbers of calls by volunteers, but employed staff need to set the example and provide guidance.

With the exception of some very small parishes, the size of a church staff almost always remains inadequate for the hospital, nursing home, and residence calls which are needed. And even in small parishes, effective outreach means that interest needs to be shown by volunteers as well as staff (generally the pastor in a small church).

Staff members who themselves make few calls should not be surprised when they find it difficult to motivate volunteers to do calling. Churches which have the most volunteers making visits almost always have a staff which makes many calls. Some calls simply need to be made by a professional from the church (given expectations in twentieth century America). As already indicated, prospective members need to have contact with volunteers and staff. Persons dealing with serious illness and other traumas generally need the outreach of a staff member and may discuss some things with a minister or other staff person that they will not with a volunteer. Routine calls by a minister provide a continuing evidence of concern which is always appreciated.

Staff members also need to provide emotional support and guidance for volunteers who do calling. Letting volunteers know that the calls are appreciated is important and being available to discuss any problems which arise helps reinforce volunteer work. Persons who have not done visiting in the past generally benefit from some instructions about how to proceed.

Remember that the pastors aren't the only professional staff members who can help your church through their calling activity. Business administrators, music directors, youth directors, religious education directors, parish visitors, and other staff members can help support the total calling program of the parish.

CONCEPT: A coordinated program of visits to every home in your parish can yield substantial benefits.

Routine calling on parish members has become relatively rare, and that fact is a tragedy. Few efforts by the church do more to increase the commitment of parish members, help church leaders stay aware of needs, bring the inactive back to parish involvement, and find prospective members as routine calls on the whole membership.

Depending on the size of your parish, such calls may only be realistic once every twelve to eighteen months and may require the involvement of both staff and volunteers. But regardless of the size of your parish, you should take seriously the possibility of a coordinated calling program that will reach every household.

Some parishes concentrate their calls on persons who have not been active. While calls on those persons are certainly important most staff members and volunteers quickly tire of making the chronically inactive the major target group for visits. Even "cold calls" on persons who have indicated no particular interest in your parish sometimes seem preferable. While the inactive members often respond positively to the call, it's still frustrating to spend considerable time visiting with people who simply do not feel the love for the church which you personally have.

It's generally much easier to do effective outreach to inactive members when they are visited as a part of a total calling program that includes many highly pleasant visits with persons who are active in the church and committed to its program. The enthusiasm generated by those visits will usually help you reach out more effectively to those who are not as active.

Unfortunately, most parishes that do "every member calling" do so only in connection with fund raising. That's not the place to begin. While the complaint that the church is only interested in the money of its members is generally not justifiable, some of our churches act in ways that give validity to the charge. Be sure that the financial drive isn't the only time members receive a call!

The chief benefit of routine calling comes precisely because the primary motivation for the call is the expression of interest and concern about the person or persons being visited. In some instances, the calling process may be made easier if those who call have literature to leave. Churches that prepare devotional materials for the Easter and Christmas seasons, for example, may find that distributing those materials by personal calls yields excellent results for the church.

Some churches use calls on the homes of members to ask their opinions through a formal or informal survey on program possibilities for the parish. Such efforts generally are very effective and yield valuable information for the church. These calls generally do not constitute a conflict with the"routine calling" described in the previous paragraph so long as there is openness to other needs in the home which may not be reflected on the survey.

When you make routine calls, use the opportunity to ask people if they have friends or neighbors who might be prospective members. You should consider personally calling on those prospective members, and your visits may encourage other members to do the same.

Some parishes organize into "neighborhood," "shepherd," or "caring" groups to make routine calling an easier task. Medium sized and large churches especially benefit from this kind of organization that places a volunteer as a "captain" or "shepherd" for a given group of homes. These volunteers can be alert throughout the year for prospective members who move into the neighborhood and for pastoral needs of members. In some urban situations, "neighborhood" may end up being defined in somewhat broad terms; but the concept continues to be useful.

Some Roman Catholic parishes are so large that the small number of priests cannot hope to visit on any routine basis in all the homes. Lay staff members and volunteers generally must assume that responsibility in such parishes. If the size of the lay staff is not sufficient to do that kind of calling, additions to that staff may be appropriate.

While most Protestant parishes benefit if volunteers as well as staff members make routine calls, staff members generally should decide on a system which lets them be a part of the routine calling process. When the "staff" consists of the pastor and the church size is relatively small, this is not a difficult task. If the church has, for example, two thousand members, the task may be more complex. A church of two thousand members, however, should have a staff of at least six full time professionals (More about staff size in chapter eight!). Two thousand members generally represent no more than nine hundred households. By simple arithmetic, that means a hundred fifty calls by each staff member will cover the membership. At five routine calls a week by each staff member, thirty weeks should be adequate to make a complete sweep. If your current staffing is only three, then sixty weeks would still accomplish the same goal.

In routine calling, don't be overly concerned about not finding particular members at home. Leaving a card or literature at the door indicates that an attempt was made and will generally have a positive effect. Keeping some kind of church records on visits to members does have importance at this point. If those records indicate that no one has been able to "complete" a call to a particular household for a long period of time, then calling by appointment may be appropriate.

Some people feel far more comfortable phoning ahead before making a routine visit. While there are some communities in which this procedure is important because of swing shifts or restrictive access to apartment and condominium complexes, remember that calls by appointment generally take much longer than"drop in" calls. And longer routine calls do not necessarily yield greater results for the church.

CONCEPT: Remember that youth, young adults, and senior citizens can make excellent representatives of the church and are great resources for routine calls.

While many young people are not emotionally prepared to help with hospital calling, they can do a very effective job helping with routine calls on parish members, visiting with nursing home residents and shut-ins, and talking with other young people about church activity. They may often be your best possibility for reaching other teens, and they are almost always well received by adults. Youth have busy lives, but many will respond positively if asked to help in visitation. Summer may provide substantial opportunity for youth involvement in outreach.

Most denominations define "young adults" as those persons between the ages of nineteen and thirty-five. In this particular instance, I am referring primarily to young adults who are attending college or other educational institutions. School breaks and summer breaks often bring back to your parish young adults who spend most of the year away from home. When they come back, some will be extremely busy catching up on visits with old friends, continuing to work on school projects, or frantically working to earn extra money. But some of them will have time available which they would be glad to share with the church. And some churches find that hiring a young adult in the summer to help with teen outreach is an excellent strategy that pays significant dividends.

Senior citizens constitute a marvelous and often overlooked resource for most churches. Many persons who have retired from the regular demands of employment have time available which they are glad to share with the church. They not only make excellent visitors to other adults but may also be outstanding youth workers! Many senior citizens are sufficiently secure in their own values not to be threatened by the struggle for identity which is so basic to many teenagers. As you develop parish strategies, remember that senior citizens may unlock great opportunities for your church.

8

STAFFING FOR GROWTH AND DECLINE

*Now in those days when the disciples were increasing in
number, the Hellenists murmured against the Hebrews because
their widows were neglected in the daily distribution. And the
twelve summoned the body of the disciples and said, "It is not
right that we should give up preaching the word of God to serve
tables. Therefore, brethren, pick out from among you seven
men of good repute, full of the Spirit and of wisdom, whom we
may appoint to this duty."*

Acts 6:1-3

While the organization of the New Testament church during the
period reported in Acts differs from what we find in most
congregations today, the spread of the church necessitated the
involvement of more people to do needed tasks. Every church has a
continuing supply of work to be done. Part can be done by
volunteers; part must be done by employed staff.

In theory, no parish needs a large employed staff. While most
denominations provide for priests or clergy to be "set apart" for
preaching and sacramental responsibilities, the continuing pastoral
care, educational ministry, administration, and outreach of the church
do not have to be done by full time clergy. Certainly lay employees
can do a large number of tasks, but the issue goes deeper: one can
make a strong argument that almost all the work in the parish should
be done by volunteers rather than employed staff. The Protestant
Reformation emphasized the "priesthood of all believers." Yet most
Protestant churches are fully as dependent on ordained clergy (and
other employed staff) as Catholic churches.

There are several reasons for the situation in which we find
ourselves. First the massive amount of work which must be done in
virtually any parish (even if the parish is declining in membership)
could only be done by volunteers if someone were available to do
massive coordination of the tasks. And no matter how great the
coordination, it would sometimes be difficult to have the right
persons available at the right times.

Second, professional skills make a difference for many jobs. Clergy
obviously possess background in administrative ministry and in
theological and Biblical study which are needed by the church. When

a church reaches sufficient size, having a staff member with considerable knowledge in Christian education enables additional program opportunities. Elaborate music programs are difficult without someone with significant musical background. Church business administrators oversee the responsible use of church resources; and a church large enough to employee a business administrator has a substantial number of "business" transactions each day.

Third, in North American culture, we've come to "expect" (rightly or wrongly, as the case may be!) certain kinds of leadership from pastors, religious educators, youth workers, music directors, church secretaries, business administrators, and so forth. While volunteers making hospital calls have significant impact, many people who are hospitalized do not feel the same about a volunteer call as about a call from a minister or priest. The same is true in many other areas of the church.

The combined weight of these factors means that our churches are very dependent on the quality of the employed staff. While that may not represent the ideal situation, it nevertheless represents the reality with which we must work. Churches with an average attendance greater than 150-200 must take staff issues very seriously if they want to grow in membership and attendance.

CONCEPT: A church which is understaffed will not grow.

While there may be a few exceptions, the generalization remains valid. Most churches need the vision, leadership, and energy of employed staff in order to reach out in ways that result in growth. A pastor who is exhausted by pressing tasks each day will have considerable trouble providing that vision and leadership (to say nothing of the ENERGY!). Some churches are so understaffed that basic pastoral care needs are neglected, and it is next to impossible for a church which does inadequate pastoral care to grow.

Consider the situations which follow. While each of these parishes no doubt has other barriers to church growth, staffing problems have major implications in each instance.

1. Faith Church has 711 adult members and an average worship attendance of 236. The congregation is twenty-four years old and had spectacular growth during the first ten years. While the community in which the church is located continues to grow, the church itself does not. In fact, membership was a little higher five years ago than today. The staff of the church consists of one horribly overworked

pastor, a full time secretary, and a part time music director (eight hours a week). The church has recognized for at least ten years that another professional staff member was needed, but there just never seems to be enough money in the budget. The pastor has responsibility for two worship services on Sunday morning, most of the youth programming, all administration, hospital calling, home visitation, and work with boards and committees. Much of his schedule is dictated by the calendar with set meetings and appointments. He continually feels as though he has to choose between making calls on prospective members and taking good care of the pastoral needs of those who already belong to the church. While his sermons are popular, he feels personally frustrated because he knows he is only spending six hours a week on sermon preparation and could do a much better job with twelve to fifteen hours a week available.

2. St. Andrew's Parish has fifteen hundred families, a parochial school serving grades one through eight and a heavy mass schedule each week. A recent study of mass attendance indicated a weekly average of 950. Two priests,a full time parish education director (separate from the parochial school staff), and a business administrator have the responsibility for everything except the parochial school. Most would describe the parochial school as underfunded but adequately staffed. Some secretarial help is available. The younger of the two priests is extremely popular in the community and has had to decline invitations to serve on numerous community groups. Just taking care of the heavy worship schedule, parish meetings, weddings, and funerals has the priests in an almost constant state of exhaustion. Parish membership has tended to go up and down with the community population, but attendance at mass and at church events stands as far less than leaders want.

3. First Church has 2,500 adult members and an average worship attendance of 475. The professional staff includes a senior pastor, two associate pastors, and a part-time minister of visitation. The minister of visitation is retired and normally only works ten hours a week. While the community in which the church is located has not declined in population, the church itself has lost members for the last fifteen years and shows no signs of growth.

While a full analysis of each church would involve far more detail than reported here, some well chosen staff additions would make a tremendous difference in each situation. Various authorities on church administration have proposed a range of suggestions for how much professional staff is "adequate" at a given level. By professional staff, I mean employed clergy, Christian educators, youth workers, parish visitors, music directors, and business administrators. The table provided here represents my own opinion, assuming that all other factors stay constant. I'm basing these around average attendance at the main worship service (or services) each week rather than on church membership, since churches count members in so many different ways.

Average Attendance	Staff Needed To Hold	Staff Needed To Grow
150	1	1½
200	1½	2
300	2	2½
400	3	4
500	4	5
600	5	6
700	6	7

You can identify many other "systems" for determining needed professional staff, but this at least provides some guidelines for you. Faith Church unquestionably needs another professional staff person to be able to grow. First Church with an average attendance of almost 500 (and a membership so large that the average attendance itself should be much higher) probably needs the equivalent of two more full time professional staff members. St. Andrew's Parish goes completely off the scale. While the fact that parochial school staff no doubt indirectly help with some functions that the church staff would otherwise do, it's no wonder the priests feel exhausted. While Catholic parishes tend not to have as large staffs as Protestant parishes, St. Andrew's clearly could benefit from a larger lay professional staff.

CONCEPT: When professional staff is increased, volunteer staff

should also increase.

The result of more staff should not be that less is done by lay volunteers. The involvement of another professional staff member should generate more programming and a greater need for volunteers. In fact, most churches do find that increases in staff make it easier to gain volunteer help. Most volunteers need a certain amount of reinforcement and guidance from employed staff. If a church has an inadequate number of employed staff, it may well have an inadequate number of volunteer staff as well.

CONCEPT: The church secretary may be the single most important staff member with the possible exception of the pastor.

Most church secretaries play an integral role in the life of the church, including the image others have of the church and its leadership. Does the secretary enthusiastically provide the needed information when people call with questions about worship services or educational opportunities?

Does the secretary try to obtain follow up information on persons who visit the church building or ask for information on the church?

Does the secretary help protect the pastor's time when necessary but also show good judgment when crises arise?

Does the secretary present the image desired when people visit the church?

Does the secretary understand and feel good about the basic beliefs and values reflected by your church?

Does the secretary have pride in the appearance of the bulletin and printed materials?

Does the secretary respect the confidentiality of persons who visit the pastor and of persons who may share problems directly with the secretary?

Does the secretary use the "power" which information provides to help the church or to build a personal power base which makes people overly dependent?

CONCEPT: All church staff members tend to be underpaid; secretaries and custodians are generally in the worst situation.

Churches are not known for high pay. Professional staff members experience that reality, and support staff (secretaries and custodians) experience it in the extreme. The support staff has a great deal to do with the church's image. A good custodian and a good secretary are in unique positions to help the church grow. They can also do considerable harm to the church. Compensation needs to be fairly based in relationship to other positions in the community. The church should ideally pay better than community organizations and businesses; certainly the church should not pay worse.

CONCEPT: Higher pay for church staff members can actually correlate positively with parish growth.

Repeated studies make it clear that longer tenure for church staff members is healthy for the local church. The fifth through eighth years are often the most productive for clergy and other professional staff members. Yet many denomination have an average tenure far below that.

While many other issues are involved, the truth remains that many church employees move to other churches or to other positions under economic pressure. They need more money. If they can advance reasonably in salary without moving, most are happy to stay far longer.

Obviously some people are ineffective and should be asked to look for other employment! But for every instance like that, there are many others in which longer tenure would do good things for the parish and the community.

While much can be said about church employees not wanting to put too much importance on what they are paid, the truth remains that such statements generally come from those who are not church employees! In the society in which we live, most people, no matter how committed to the church, have trouble separating their own worth from the financial compensation which they receive. Better paid staff members tend to feel better about themselves and tend as a result to do better work for the parish.

9

Ministerial Style and Church Growth

*Now John wore a garment of camel's hair, and a leather girdle
around his waist; and his food was locusts and wild honey.
They went out to him Jerusalem and all Judea and all the
region about the Jordan, and they were baptized by him in the
river Jordan, confessing their sins.*

Matthew 3:4-6

John Simmons projects warmth to everyone he meets. People with
no church home often ask him to officiate at their weddings and
perform funeral services for their loved ones. During his seven years
at St. Paul's Church, many members have been added because of
admiration and affection for John. When asked what is unique about
his pastoral style and why he is so popular, John is unable to identify
anything unique. He cares deeply about people, but he doesn't feel he
cares any more deeply than most clergy he knows. John, however,
feels very comfortable with people; and expressing his concern to
others is a natural, almost intuitive response.

Beth Newbury has been associate minister at First Church for three
years. It was her first position after seminary, and she was the first
woman pastor for that congregation. Beth cares deeply for people
but, unlike John Simmons, is not quite so comfortable with them. She
needs time to grow close to people, and she initially had anxiety
about doing that on the staff of such a large congregation. The fears
were needless. While the initial five or six months were a little rocky,
she's grown very comfortable with the congregation; and they are
deeply impressed with her.

Ben Armstrong, like John and Beth, cares deeply for people.
Unfortunately for his ministry, Ben has a quick temper and can easily
feel slighted., Though he considers it a spiritual failing, he sometimes
can't help "blowing up" at church members (and the church
hierarchy) over differences of opinion. He always apologizes
afterward, and many people appreciate the fact that Ben doesn't
compromise his opinions or hide his emotions. Nevertheless, some
people are intimidated by his stormy style and unwilling to approach
him about anything that might trigger his temper. While some people
drop out of activity following a confrontation with Ben, more persons
simply avoid activity because they don't want to risk confrontation.

Ben is a very dedicated pastor and always has many strong supporters, but no church he has pastored has sustained growth even though demographics encouraged growth in three of the five parishes he has served.

John, Beth, and Ben share concern for people and commitment to Christ. All three are hard working and love the church passionately. Yet their personalities or styles of ministry unquestionably affect the growth potential in their churches. Can Ben change his personality and in so doing help the church? I doubt it. In fact I know Ben (though that isn't his real name, of course) very well; and love his passion for life and the strong stands he takes on mission and social issues.

John the Baptist, dressed in camel's hair and a leather girdle, must have been a striking figure even by first century standards. I suspect that some contemporary churches would be reluctant to let John in the front door – let alone hire him as a pastor! Yet people from Jerusalem and all Judea came to hear John preach and were baptized by him in the river Jordan.

We must be careful about setting standards on ministerial (and other employed staff) personality and style. I want to share some concepts which may be helpful, but I do so with a certain amount of anxiety. Our God uses people in ways we would never anticipate and often draws straight paths with the crooked lines of our lives. My focus in this chapter will not be on personality but on styles of ministry. Only God and the individual involved can determine when changes should be made in one's personality, and only God's grace can make such change possible. There are some styles of ministry which contribute to church growth; and John, Beth, and Ben can all make changes in style if convinced doing so will benefit Christ's work.

CONCEPT: Ministers and other staff need to be aware of how they are perceived by members of the congregation.

John, Beth, and Ben may not be able to change much about their personalities; but they can benefit in knowing how they "come across" to others. A wide gap sometimes exists between an individual's perception of himself or herself and how other persons view that individual.

When I served in an administrative capacity for my denomination, I often found myself attempting to negotiate better understanding between clergy and the people they served. In an especially tense church board meeting, I saw a pastor turn red in the face, hit the table with the palm of his hand so hard that two people literally jumped out of their seats, and yell: "I am not an angry person! I am always calm and in control." A few moments later an elderly woman commented: "Well, Pastor, if you ever do think you're going to lose control, please warn me. I'd want to be a long distance away." The pastor wept later in the meeting as he discovered that many church members were bothered by his volatility. He truly did not perceive himself that way and actually thought he was always in firm control of his emotions.

While the preceding example is an extreme one, it's nevertheless true that our self-perceptions on behavior are not always accurate. Church members are often very considerate of the feelings of their pastor and are reluctant to share criticism. Church staff should be intentional about soliciting feedback.

Most churches have a pastor parish committee, personnel committee, or other organization concerned with staff matters. A minister or other professional staff member should cultivate a style of relating to that committee which encourages members to share feedback which will help. Some clergy find it useful to share a simple form within committee members and ask them to complete and return the form anonymously. The same form could be used with members of another governing board or with selected congregation members. An example follows.

I care deeply about the church and its members. I like to check at times to see how members of the church perceive me. Your honest answers to these questions will help me conduct a better ministry. Please add any comments you would like. The sheet can be slipped under my office door, and you should not put your name on it unless you want to talk with me about some of the items. Indicate the strength of your agreement with each statement by a number from "1" (low agreement) to "5" (high agreement).

_____ 1. You seem to me to be very concerned about members of the church.

_____ 2. I have always felt that you liked me personally and cared about my well-being.

_____ 3. I think most members of the church believe you care about them.

_____ 4. You project warmth to people as you relate to them in the life of the church.

_____ 5. You don't have any habits which are annoying or offensive to members. (If there are such habits, please specify them on the reverse side.)

_____ 6. To the extent I am aware of this, I think you project a positive image to persons in the community who are not members of our church.

_____ 7. I am impressed by your knowledge of the names and family situations of members of the parish.

_____ 8. I would feel comfortable coming to you if I had a serious problem to discuss.

_____ 9. I think most members would feel comfortable coming to you if they had a serious problem to discuss.

_____ 10. You are easy to reach or leave a message for when people need you.

_____ 11. When people share individual problems or church program needs with you, you always listen carefully and do your best to respond.

_____ 12. You never belittle people or make them feel foolish for something they've said or done.

_____ 13. You display considerable patience in working with others.

_____ 14. You sometimes are too reluctant to share your opinion on church decisions.

_____ 15. You sometimes try too hard to push your own ideas or projects through the church.

_____ 16. When you promise to do something for others, you follow through and accomplish it.

Other comments:

Obviously the form may need some modification for each pastor and church, but you can readily tailor it to your situation. Music directors, Christian educators, business administrators, youth workers, and parish visitors can modify the form for their own use.

Note that although personality obviously influences how people perceive ministers and other staff, the questions in the survey are intended to get at matters of style. When a pastor genuinely cares about others but is not perceived as caring, it's time for some evaluation. Persons who do not come across as caring may want to think about considerations such as these:

_____ Do you look people in the eye when you talk to them? Doing so helps people feel that your attention is focused on them. Don't engage in staring contests, but do remember the value of eye contact.

_____ Do you appear at ease and not under tension when you talk to people? It's easy to be thinking so hard about the next task to complete that one isn't actually focusing on the conversation at hand. This often shows in one's appearing uneasy and tense during a conversation.

_____ Do you focus on what people are saying to you? It's easy to get caught worrying so much about how people perceive you that you miss what they have to say.

_____ If you really are too busy to talk with someone, do you set a future time to do so? This can be especially important on a hectic Sunday morning when many people have things to check with church staff members. Make a habit of writing down the names of people you need to contact later in the week whether you set a specific appointment or not.

_____ When someone shares a concern or problem, do you ask them later how things are going? "My mother is in the hospital in Idaho." "My son is having trouble getting along with a teacher." When someone shares such a problem, make a calendar note to ask about it later. Of course you might visit the hospitalized mother (even though not a member of your parish) if you live in Idaho; but even if you live in Georgia, you can ask the person how his or her mother is doing.

_____ When people share a concern that seems frivolous or silly to you, do you still give them your full attention and avoid belittling comments? "the choir sounded a little off key today." "Did you know that debtors was misspelled in the bulletin?" "Someone hasn't returned a book to the church library." It's easy to unthinkingly destroy the enthusiasm of others. When people share concerns that are frivolous, you obviously shouldn't share agreement you don't feel or criticize another church worker, but you can listen carefully and express thanks for the concern being shared even if nothing can be done.

Changes in style are possible and can help. Of course personality does influence style. When a personality trait is so strong that a change in style isn't realistic, then be honest with people about the limitation. Ben Armstrong, for example, has learned to talk openly with his personnel committee about his struggles with his temper. Committee members help interpret that to others and help people see that Ben's temper is a result of his passion for life, which is a strength.

CONCEPT: Clergy need to place major priority on visiting members and potential members in their homes and in hospitals.

I've emphasized visiting so much in this book that I must sound like a broken record! Nothing communicates pastoral concern more clearly than visiting a member or potential member at his or her home or in the hospital. Other staff members and laity certainly should make such visits, but nothing replaces those visits from clergy given the particular way in which clergy are viewed as representing the church.

I write these words acutely aware of the reality that some priests are so overworked that routine visits may be out of the question. In those parishes, lay employees and volunteers must assume most of that responsibility.

Senior pastors of some large Protestant churches may feel that routine calling is as impossible for them as for their counterparts in the Catholic Church. Since there are other ministers on the staff, I urge churches to shift staff priorities in ways which make possible at least some routine calls by the senior pastor in hospitals and homes. In a large church obviously the senior pastor can carry only a small portion of that responsibility, but his or her calls will have significant impact. Word travels fast, and a pastor who visits people is always talked about as a concerned pastor.

CONCEPT: **Ministers need to recognize important events in the lives of people.**

Edith Merrell is eighty-six years old and lives alone. She's been blessed with good health but has outlived her husband and one of her children. She was deeply touched on her birthday by a short, handwritten note from her pastor. The note took five minutes of the pastor's time and became Edith's chief topic of conversation for a week.

Samuel Clay's world fell apart with the death of his wife a year ago. While his friends reached out to him strongly at the time of the funeral, their lives have moved on; and they aren't aware of the enormous pain which is still so real to him. He was greatly helped on the first anniversary of her death to find his minister at his front door. The visit was a short one but reaffirmed the pastor's concern and gave Samuel opportunity to share feelings he hadn't expressed before.

The clergy involved gave good pastoral care to Edith and Samuel. Edith's pastor has learned the value of writing to members on their birthdays. Pastors of extremely large congregations may find that practice overwhelming but can do so for older members of the church who most need that contact. Samuel's minister makes frequent calendar notation to help him remember significant events in the lives of church members. He not only remembers with compassion the anniversaries of deaths but also with joy the anniversaries of weddings and confirmations. He always calls on every young person in his church on the first anniversary of that person having joined the congregation.

Edith and Samuel are goodwill ambassadors not just for their pastors but for their churches. For the most part church staff are not aware of significant events in the lives of nonmembers and thus can't response to them in the same way. The pastor who shows this kind of concern for members does develop a positive reputation for his or her pastoral work, and that reputation spreads to potential members.

CONCEPT: **Ministers and other professional staff should follow up quickly on information about potential members and share that information with appropriate individuals and groups in the parish.**

June and Mark Whitley moved to Summerville and attended St. Matthew's their second sunday in town. On the following Monday, a lay person from the parish visited in their home and learned that their son was entering the hospital the next day for medical tests. The lay person called the pastor who visited June, Mark, and their son at the hospital.

Bob Weston, the minister of the West Side Community Parish, made a routine visit to the James family following their attendance at a worship service. The next day he called the choir director who invited Mrs. James to attend rehearsal; a Sunday school teacher who invited Mr. and Mrs. James to his class; and the president of the youth group who arranged transportation for the two teenage children to the Sunday evening youth group.

A member of the choir at First Church called the minister after a rehearsal and told her that a woman who has been singing in the choir had asked questions about joining the church. The woman had been reluctant to join because her husband belonged to another congregation, but she wasn't comfortable worshiping in her husband's church. The pastor visited the woman to tell her more about the church and answer her questions, being careful not to put pressure on her about membership and to affirm that the church was very pleased to have her participating in the choir. The pastor called back the choir member who had contacted her and suggested continued warmth to the woman but care that she not be made to feel any pressure to join the congregation. It was clear that pressure would be counterproductive and not in the spirit of Christlike acceptance.

In each of the three instances just described, the potential members became members. The woman whose husband belonged to another church did not become a member for a long time, but eventually she and her husband both joined.

In each instance the pastors involved worked cooperatively with other members of the congregation. They acted on information given them about potential members; they shared information with people and groups in the church who could help potential members feel welcome.

The third pastor, dealing with a sensitive situation, was especially careful not to make the choir participant feel any pressure about membership. The pastor shared the church's pleasure in having the woman involved, answered questions openly, but did not push for any change in member status. People dealing with family differences in religious matters generally react negatively to any kind of pressure. The pastor and the choir members created an open, accepting climate which made the woman and finally her husband as well comfortable in the church.

While it's possible to overwhelm and thus threaten potential members with too many contacts, that is rarely the problem in most churches. As long as the contacts are affirming rather than aggressive, potential members almost always respond positively. Most of us have a shyness or reticence about new situation. Even persons who outwardly seem to have great self-confidence may be compensating for inner anxiety and the fear of not fitting into a particular situation. The more initiatives a church takes to help people feel welcome, the more likely that those persons will become active members.

Clergy and other professional staff can't carry the full load of member contact and recruitment, but they have a vital role to play because of the importance their contact with potential members represents and because staff can be valuable links with the others in the parish helping in member recruitment. Clergy who share information and act on information about potential members reinforce similar actions in parish members.

CONCEPT: Ministers should share positive feedback with those who help bring in members.

It seems obvious, but one of the most important roles clergy can play in membership recruitment is that of sharing positive feedback with others who play major roles in that process. Acting on information from church school teachers, lay visitors, choir members, and others is itself strong reinforcement. People also like to be thanked for their involvement – by phone call, letter, or occasionally even personal visit.

Anna Meadows belongs to First Church. She retired three years ago from her position as a public school teacher, but she certainly hasn't retired from her church membership! She's one of the most tireless workers of the church. She voluntarily maintains attendance records and also makes personal visits to many potential members. At least twice a year, her pastor takes her out for lunch as a way of expressing appreciation for her work and as an opportunity to seek her suggestions for improving the church's member recruitment.

Bob Harley pastors a large church which has an excellent program of "member sponsors." The church evangelism committee assigns a couple or a single person to each potential member. The sponsors see that potential members are aware of the programs of the church and feel welcome in the church community. They often share Sunday brunch with potential members. Each time new persons join the church, Bob takes a few minutes to send a handwritten note of thanks to the sponsors involved. The church has an annual banquet for new members and their sponsors, which is another important affirmation.

CONCEPT: Ministers should help church members become more comfortable talking about their faith and reaching out to nonmembers.

Many people are truly not comfortable talking about their faith in Christ. They faith may be deep, but they find it awkward to express it verbally. While some persons feel their faith is so personal that they don't want to talk about it, most would like to feel more comfortable discussing faith issues.

Clergy, trained by education and experience to talk about matters of faith, can provide important help to church members in this area. It is very difficult for people to witness effectively to others when they aren't comfortable talking about personal beliefs.

Ministers and other staff can help people in this process in many ways:

1. By acting as resource persons and helping train volunteer visitors or member sponsors.

2. By forming study groups using a resource like *Plain Talk About Church Growth* (especially the "Thirty Day Experiment" in the final chapter).

3. By encouraging all kinds of Bible study and spiritual life groups in the parish. While these groups aren't focused on member recruitment, the experiences in these groups help people feel more comfortable talking about their faith.

4. By using the pulpit to encourage people to share their faith and by the provision of practical suggestions to help in that process.

5. By making it clear that they are available as resource persons about spiritual matters and always willing to talk with people about matters of personal faith. This should seem an obvious item, but people sometimes are reluctant to seek such help out of fear of appearing foolish. Ministers can let people know through the pulpit and groups that there are no foolish questions where matters of faith are concerned.

CONCEPT: Ministers and other professional staff should be encouraged to have involvement in community organizations.

Every member of the church, of course, represents the church in the community. Ministers, however, are representatives of the church in a special way. The minister who is a respected member of Kiwanis, Rotary, Lion's Club, Jaycees, Business and Professional Women, or a similar organization may increase the esteem in which the minister's church is held. When the minister has little or no community involvement, the implication may be that the minister is not concerned about matters outside the congregation.

The potential for community involvement is just as large for clergy and other church staff as for anyone else:

- Service clubs such as those listed above
- United Fund
- Chamber of Commerce
- P.T.A.
- Other school organizations
- YMCA and YWCA
- Scouting organizations
- Musical groups
- Self-help groups
- Telephone counseling services
- College and university organizations
- Hospital and health care organizations
- Cystic fibrosis and similar organizations
- Organizations for the handicapped
- Red Cross and similar agencies
- Ecumenical church groups

And so the list can be continued. Some authorities believe that it's especially important for clergy to belong to "prestigious" service organizations. I'm not willing to make such a statement. Great good can come out of ministerial involvement with any community organization, and my own opinion is that clergy should seek those areas of participation which are attractive to them personally and consistent with their own values.

Clergy occasionally do become so involved with a particular community project that they neglect other responsibilities. Those situations, however, involve only a small minority of clergy. The community activity of most clergy creates a better image for the church and should be encouraged.

While the purpose of community involvement by clergy should be service to others and personal fulfillment, that involvement inevitably opens opportunities in member recruitment. Persons with no church home will seek out clergy they know through the community when at a point of personal or spiritual crisis or need. Clergy can and should respond positively to those opportunities. The minister's involvement in the community likewise communicates concern about community needs, and that image is positive for the church.

10

Using the Media for Publicity

*And they all ate and were satisfied. And they took up twelve
baskets full of the broken pieces left over. And those who ate
were about five thousand men, besides women and children.*
Matthew 14:20-21

**CONCEPT: Don't expect too much from using the media to
publicize your church program.**

That's a negative way to start a chapter! But the plain truth is that
churches tend to expect too much from articles in the newspaper,
radio broadcasts of Sunday worship, and carefully placed advertising.
While all these efforts have a place, they will not bring people
flocking to the doors of your church. And they will yield almost
nothing unless you have careful plans to follow up on those who visit
your church or make inquiry about your programs as a result of
media publicity.

Over five thousand people gathered to hear Christ without the
benefit of the yellow pages, newspaper articles, radio announcements,
or television. They came because they had seen personally or heard
from others what wonderful things Christ said and did. While media
have an important role, they don't represent the most significant
impact for the local church. Skillful use of television can provide good
results on a denominational basis, for the promotion of certain
mission and benevolent ministries, and for the perpetuation of
ministries that are exclusively devoted to the television medium. Local
churches have some creative opportunities available but can also
waste a great deal of energy and money attempting to compete with
slicker projects of national television ministries.

**CONCEPT: Don't forget the yellow pages; keep your parish listed;
keep the listing current!**

People do use the yellow pages. The larger your community, the
more prospective members will make use of the yellow pages in
identifying churches to visit. Persons passing through on vacation or
those staying in a motel while preparing to move to your city will also

use the yellow pages. Even if you are in a very small community, you can expect that the yellow pages may be where newcomers turn to find out the time of worship services and religious education opportunities.

At the very least have an ad in the yellow pages which gives the name, address, and phone of your church. People will gain more from your ad if:

- It appears in a box.
- There is a small picture of your church or symbol of your denomination.
- The names of professional staff members are included.
- The times of worship services and other Sunday activities are included(with indication of any seasonal changes which are nominally made).
- Brief information is provided about other programs offered by your parish, such as day care or parochial school.

Many churches are reluctant to include times for worship and religious education classes. "The people will call the church if they're interested." Logical. But wrong. Many people have a mild phobia about telephones. They are uncomfortable making calls to people and organizations with which they are unfamiliar. People also tend not to make a decision about visiting until the evening before. At seven or eight on Saturday night most people are reluctant to call the pastor at home.

Make a significant effort to identify any special summer or winter schedules in sufficient time to include that information in the yellow pages. If that's not possible, just indicate "Summer schedule may vary" (or words to that effect). It's better to have the exact schedule for nine months of the year and leave people stuck calling for three months than to withhold the information for all twelve months.

CONCEPT: People won't come to your church if they can't find it; use signs!

Few things frustrate newcomers more than having trouble finding a church building and then experiencing frustration about which entrance to use. Consider signs as part of your church advertising effort. I'm not referring to billboards on the highway but to small signs which indicate directions from main highways or streets:

FIRST CHURCH
TURN RIGHT

ST. PAUL'S CHURCH
FIVE BLOCKS

LAKE STREET CHURCH
RIGHT AT THE CORNER
GO TWO BLOCKS
TURN LEFT

LAKE STREET CHURCH
TURN LEFT

Many denominations have signs available through church supply houses or catalogs. Using those of your own denomination can be an advantage since attractive symbols are often part of the signs.

You should also clearly mark entrances to your church. Help people know which entrance to use for worship; which for church school; which for the parish office. Tasteful metal or woods signs above or at the side of the doors can give this information without detracting from the aesthetics of your church.

CONCEPT: Use newspaper advertisements and articles.

Unless your community is extremely small or a local newspaper automatically includes a listing of church schedules in the Saturday paper, you should consider buying a small weekly advertisement. This lets people who are new to the community know about your church and also provides a subtle reminder to your own members. The ad does not have to be large, and the same guidelines for the yellow page advertisements should be considered. Some pastors feel strongly that including the sermon title helps draw interest; most of the sermon titles that I read are too boring to draw much interest. You do want to differ from the yellow page ad in one respect – whether you change sermon titles weekly or not, make periodic change in the appearance of your newspaper advertisement. That does help regular readers pay more attention to it.

Money can be a problem with newspaper ads. If you have to make a choice, keeping an advertisement in the yellow pages stands as more important (and more impact for the money) than a newspaper ad. Consider getting businesses or individuals to sponsor your newspaper advertisements. That kind of effort may build good will for a local business and provides a needed service for your church.

Most newspapers will print at least some articles submitted by your church without any charge or obligation. To increase the probability of getting articles printed:

• Get to know the religion or civic affairs editor for your newspaper (or newspapers). Take that person to lunch; have coffee together. Learn what kinds of articles are most helpful.
• Always submit articles neatly typed and double spaced. Hand written articles are significantly less likely to get printed.
• Be concise in the article. Newspaper space is valuable. Don't give extraneous information that makes the article too long.
• Be sure to include the names of people who are giving leadership. Most newspapers like to include that information.
• Include photographs when possible. Photographs are best if black and white. You should normally not expect to get the photograph back.
• Think about news of special interest to other people. Don't depend on the newspaper to announce all your internal church events. A film showing that's open to the public is of interest; a parish council meeting generally is not. A story about the church youth group doing volunteer work for a community agency will be welcome by most newspapers. A story about the trustees trimming the church bushes will only make the news if the paper is really having trouble with filler. Most newspapers are more likely to help you publicize a workshop on "Improved Parenting" than a study group about "The Sermon on the Mount." If a professor from a seminary will be a guest leader for a study group, then you may have something newsworthy.

CONCEPT: Broadcasting or televising church worship services provides a valuable ministry to invalids, but don't expect increases in membership or attendance as a result of such broadcasts.

Persons who are sick or disabled benefit greatly from worship services which are broadcast on radio or shown on regular or cable television. That fact alone gives good justification for the practice.
But with only a few exceptions, such efforts generally don "t increase attendance or membership. There are several reasons for this:

• People who are looking for a church home are not likely to be watching television or listening to radio when your services are broadcast.
• Most worship services inevitably include times of announcements, collection of the offering, and other moments that are awkward

from the standpoint of the radio or television participant. In fact the lengthy period of announcements common in most congregations is just plain deadly to anyone who isn't part of the congregation.

• High quality radio broadcasts or television productions require relatively expensive equipment and a priority on speaking and on planning the service for the media audience as much as for the persons in the congregation. Yet there are generally better uses for money than expensive equipment and the worshipping congregation should be the priority in planning.

Radio generally offers a less expensive approach than television to sharing worship services with relatively few sacrifices in the usefulness to the public. There are many other approaches to these media which can give you greater value if you want to make a more significant investment.

OTHER USES FOR RADIO, TELEVISION, AND CABLE

The discussion thus far has centered on relatively traditional approaches to church publicity through the yellow pages, newspaper ads, radio, and television. Radio and television have primarily been used by local churches to share worship services. As previously suggested, such services are very beneficial to the hospitalized and shut-ins but are not necessarily good evangelistic outreach opportunities. In this section, I want to briefly highlight some ways to use electronic media in addition to sharing worship services. These suggestions are not "original," but they may help stimulate some new directions in thinking for you.

This section's title identifies "cable" as something separate from "television." The distinction I'm attempting to make is between regular network stations which can be received with or without cable and those local stations that are broadcast only through cable and which are generally reserved for a significant amount of local programming. I'm not talking about MTV, HBO, CINEMAX, the DISNEY channel, or similar premium offerings.

The reason for the distinction involves both economics and degree of programming sophistication. Advertising or purchasing time on a regular network channel, even on a local basis, can be quite expensive. Further, the equipment and technical skill needed to have advertisements or productions which "look good" in the context of the evening news on one side and MASH reruns on the other is very high. Churches should carefully assess the extent to which such expensive programming and advertising is appropriate in a world filled with hungry people.

Local cable channels, however, offer some unique opportunities. Many have equipment available if programming is done in the studio, and some cable stations will provide a fair amount of technical help without charge. While high quality productions are still important, comparisons to programming on that channel will be made with other locally produced shows which have been done largely by nonprofit and community organizations. That's still not an excuse for sloppy work (and people won't watch sloppy productions with any consistency), but it can make for pragmatic advantages.

Churches which want to televise worship services from the sanctuary can quickly spend well in excess of a hundred thousand dollars on video equipment for the sanctuary. In addition, the televising of those services on a local network station will be a rather high continuing weekly expense. A church produced show about local hunger needs, however, can be done with high quality using equipment at the cable station and with perhaps no fee at all. That's a big difference.

Consider the following ideas and see what additional ones you and others in your church can generate.

1. Advertise on the radio. Rates are favorable, and production can be done at the station. Emphasize warmth and concern for people in talking about what your parish has to offer.

2. Advertise on television. For advertisements, local cable channels are generally not a good option. Unless the channel has regular programming, people simply won't be tuned to it to see your advertisement. The greatest success with church advertisements on television seems to come with thirty to sixty second spots shown just before, during, or after the local news in the early evening (supper time) or late at night (10 P.M. or 11 P.M.).

3. Consider using an advertisement provided by your denomination. Your church avoids significant production costs but has a high quality advertisement. Those which are "human interest" attention-getters are particularly good.   (The Mormons have produced some excellent advertisements in this category.)

4. If you produce your own advertisement, pay the extra money to obtain help from an advertising agency that has experience in producing television ads. If you are going to pay high rates for a thirty to sixty second spot, you want the quality to be excellent.

5. Take advantage of public service meditation time on radio and television stations. These are generally coordinated through a local ministerial association.

6. Sponsor your own early morning or late evening meditation time on a local network station. This can be a time as brief as two to five minutes and can generally be coordinated with a station's own schedule, especially late in the evening. (The alternative to a two to five minute spot is generally a thirty minute program, which is expensive.)

7. Cooperate with your denomination in getting denominational programs on your local stations. Many denominations, including the Southern Baptists, Roman Catholics, and United Methodists, have produced some outstanding programs for use on network channels. Work cooperatively to get these aired on public service time or to arrange local sponsors. You church will benefit from the positive image that these productions create for the denomination.

8. Create a weekly "talk show" on a cable channel. While considerable time must be invested to make these good experiences, the out of pocket cost for production will generally be minimal. You need to do such a show on a regular basis if you want to have much impact, and you should schedule the show before or after another locally produced show. That maximizes the probability of people in addition to parish members seeing the program. Provide additional publicity about the program through newspaper advertisements and fliers. Talk about tonics of importance to people:

- Building a stronger personal faith
- Coping with the loss of a loved one
- Dealing with serious illness
- Raising children
- Helping teens with sexuality issues
- Confronting the world hunger problem
- Responsibly using television in the home
- Reviewing popular records and motion pictures
- Developing greater self-confidence

And so the list could continue. Choose topics in which many people will be interested and bring a Christian perspective to those topics. You will draw the interest of many people who may in turn become interested in your parish. But be certain you do careful preparation of these shows.

9. Involve young people in producing a regular cable show. Teens may find considerable enjoyment in doing their own show once a week, and both teens and adults will watch youth produced programs.

10. Broadcast "thoughts for the day" on a popular radio station.

11. Sponsor a special Lenten series on regular T.V. or on a cable channel. Both Protestants and Roman Catholics can find considerable meaning in the well produced "INSIGHT" films from the Paulist fathers. Do heavy local publicity, and encourage neighborhood discussion groups. Use these as opportunities to reach out to nonmembers living near members of your parish.

12. If you are going to televise your worship services (on regular television or cable), then be prepared to spend the money to do the job right! Have high quality video equipment, improve the acoustics of your sanctuary if necessary, and have persons with the needed technical skills present. You should also consider arranging your service of worship in such a way that parish announcements and the collection of the offering do not have to be televised. You may even find that you can televise thirty minutes of your worship service that includes a preparatory hymn, the Scripture reading, the sermon or homily, and then a final hymn. That will lower the amount of time you have to purchase and may well improve audience reaction to he show.

Printing, Mail, and Church Growth

*Paul, called by the will of God to be an apostle of Christ Jesus,
and our brother Sosthenes, To the church of God which is at
Corinth, to those sanctified in Christ Jesus . . .*
1 Corinthians 1: 1-2a

Paul conducted part of his ministry by letters to congregations, and written communications have continued as an important part of the church's work. Most of our churches routinely use the mail service in a broad range of ways:

- the letters which many churches send to parish visitors
- "we missed you" cards to those who have been absent
- "get well" or "happy birthday" cards which some classes and groups sent to members
- the funding requests which go out by mail
- the announcements of committee meetings
- the parish newsletter
- informal notes received by the pastor and other staff
- notes by the pastor and other staff
- transfers of membership sent through the mail
- the wide assortment of direct mail offers which churches receive (one of which probably caused you to order this book)

As you go through the mail you receive each week and examine the mail that goes out from the church, you could add to the above list. We do use the mail extensively.

But we do not always use it well. In this chapter, I want to highlight ways to improve the church's use of print materials and to share some ways to use print materials for direct membership recruitment. I don't want to give a false expectation; using the mails creatively alone won't cause anyone to join your church. But direct mail publicity can help you find prospective members.

CONCEPT: Don't send mimeographed or photocopied letters to persons who have visited your church or to persons who have been absent from worship or classes.

Many churches recognize the value of writing to those who have visited worship services. Many also use cards or letters as an attempt to communicate with those members who have missed worship or classes. Using obviously mimeographed or photocopied letters can completely destroy whatever good might be accomplished by these communications. We live in an age of form letters. We expect them from many institutions and for many reasons. If your credit card company or a department store actually bothers to send you an individually typed, personally signed letter, it probably means that you're seriously behind on your payments! (That's one way to get personalized attention from secular society, but it only works if you get very, very far behind.)

And we anticipate form communications from the church for meeting reminders, financial information, usher instructions, and other purposes. But a visitor to worship certainly is not going to be impressed by a mimeographed or photocopied letter. And someone who has been absent can hardly feel "missed" by receiving an obviously form reminder. People do notice the difference.

There are only so many things you can say in a letter to a visitor or in a note to someone who has been absent. I'm not arguing for unlimited creativity; none of us have that. But I am arguing for individually typed and personally signed letters and notes for the two purposes mentioned in this concept. It's better for the communication to be short and individually prepared than to be long and photocopied.

Churches which have a high volume of visitors should purchase a computer or word processing equipment so that the individual letters can be prepared without having to be individually typed. That's one of the marvels of our electronic society. You can store the text of letters in the computer and then just insert the appropriate name and address. Even in a very large church, an efficient computer system means that a secretary can prepare the letters to visitors very quickly; and signing those will only take a few seconds or minutes of a pastor's time. Some software programs are so sophisticated that names and addresses of people by categories can actually be inserted into letters once those names and addresses have been entered the first time.

The benefit of the word processing program can be quickly lost however, if the letters and envelopes are prepared on a low quality dot matrix printer. If you invest the money in a computer system for your church, spend enough for a high quality dot matrix printer or a letter quality printer. And not all dot matrix printers which call themselves "high quality" actually are. Look at print samples carefully. In most instances, you'll find that a letter quality printer is worth the extra price. Laser printers may become good options as their prices fall.

Another point needs to be made concerning letters to persons who have been absent. Individually prepared letters or notes are of considerably greater worth than photocopied or pre-printed letters. Hand written notes from teachers or other class members are even better. But no written communication is the ideal way to reach out to someone who has been absent. If that person was absent because of sickness or personal problems, then that individual needs the personal contact of a phone call or visit. If that person is unhappy with the church about something, you'll never discover the problem by sending a letter. It's far better to make a phone call shortly after the break in attendance pattern and then to follow up the phone call with a visit to the home if attendance is not resumed.

And a letter to a visitor at worship should only be a preliminary step in reaching out to that person. A visit from a staff member or volunteer should happen within a few days of the visit. The letter is generally appreciated, and the time for preparing the letter is not wasted. But the letter won't bring the person into membership.

CONCEPT: Poorly prepared print materials reflect badly on the church; both prospective and inactive members will be more critical than those who are active in the church.

You don't have to use professional typesetting and layout for newsletters, brochures about your church, and other information which must be prepared in large quantities. Most people respond very well to typewritten copy.

But there's no excuse for messy copy! By that I mean:

- newsletters, brochures, and other information with obviously misspelled words and grammatical errors.
- pictures which are badly out of focus.
- drawings which are poorly done.
- ink splotches on the printed pages.
- copy that is poorly spaced and looks unattractive on the page.

And that's how many church newsletters, brochures, and letters look. Active members may not be critical of such errors. In fact those who are active in the church may in time become so accustomed to errors in printed communications that they cease to notice them.

But prospective members and inactive members notice them. And they may well wonder how much pride the church has if it is willing to send out sloppy looking material. You can help the situation readily by having someone who is skilled at proofing copy for spelling and grammatical errors go through anything the church is preparing to print. Use a good quality typewriter for preparing communications. If you have a church mimeograph that is held together by paper clips and chewing gum, put the poor machine out of its misery and seek contributions for a new one or share the use of one with a business or another church.

CONCEPT: Direct mail publicity and surveys can be an excellent but expensive way to identify potential members for your parish.

Direct mall publicity and surveys never will be as effective as house to house canvasses and invitations to attend church which are shared by active members. But these approaches can be beneficial, especially in rapidly growing communities.

Check with your post office, realtors, and mailing services to find out about lists of households which are available for your community. Then take one of two basic approaches:

1. Develop direct mail publicity which highlights the things which you think are distinctive about your parish. Send that to persons in a particular neighborhood along with a card to return if people would like to be contacted for further information about your parish.

2. Send a survey to the people in a given neighborhood. Ask people to identify their church affiliation, if any, and include other questions about their religious concerns and interests. Provide an envelope for them to return the survey to your church. From those returns, you'll find prospective members.

Some guidelines can help you in developing and using such materials:

• Always include a letter in the mailing. People read copy in a letter with more care than they read a brochure, no matter how attractive the brochure may be.

• Always include a response card or envelope. Otherwise you won't get a response.

• Determine what your response will be when people indicate

a desire for more information about your church or when
they indicate that they do not have a church home. You will
usually want to think in terms of a visit to that person's
home, though you may also want to have a letter and
brochure to mail. Keep in mind that you need several stages
of response: perhaps a letter, followed by a visit followed
by another visit.

• Keep the tone of what you send positive. Saying or implying
negative things about other churches always ends up
working against you. In the long run, you always benefit
by being positive.

• Make it clear that you aren't trying to take members away
from other churches. When you send to an entire
neighborhood or your whole community, you obviously
are going to reach many people who already are active in a
local church. You want to make it clear that you are not
wanting to take members from another church. You want
to reach persons who are not members of a church, and
(in the event of a survey) you want to learn more about
the needs of your community.

• Don't mail just before a major holiday; your material
will get tossed aside.

I also want to emphasize that direct mail approaches are relatively
expensive in comparison to volunteer canvasses. They are, however,
a way to quickly spread a great deal of information about your parish.
Through surveys, you can also learn a lot about your community.

12

WORSHIP STRATEGIES

*And as soon as he came near the camp and saw the calf and
the dancing, Moses' anger burned hot, and he threw the tables
out of his hands and broke them at the foot of the mountain.*
Exodus 32:20

Worship doesn't automatically bring blessings. It obviously didn't
for the Hebrew people who mistakenly directed their worship at the
golden calf instead of toward God who had led them away from
Pharaoh and cared for their needs. Moses broke the tablets in anger,
and the punishment of the people which followed seems severe to
those of us in the twentieth century for whom "idolarty" has become
far more subtle and sophisticated. (Money, success, political parties,
jobs, cars, and houses are among our modern idols.)

Worship services in most of our churches end up having many
purposes in addition to that of giving praise to God and seeking
guidance for our daily lives. You and I are familiar with the mixed
motivations out of which worship services are constructed and with
which people come to share. We know, for example:

• That many people evaluate the worship service by its
"entertainment" level.

• That the beauty (and sometimes the expense) of the sanctuary
has an impact on some persons.

• That many people are centered on their own needs rather than
looking toward God.

• That those of us who lead services of worship are often more
concerned with how we "come across" than with being a part of the
act of worship ourselves.

• That the quality of the music provided by organist, choir, and
others will be evaluated by many in attendance rather than simply
accepted as part of our offering to God.

• That people are often preoccupied with how they are dressed
and with what time the roast comes out of the oven at home rather
than with worship.

• That some people have come for the purpose of being seen by
others and are thinking very little about the service of worship as
such.

And so the list could be continued! Given all those realities, I am in some ways reluctant to suggest lots of specific improvements in worship out of fear that doing so reinforces some of the mixed motivations which are already present.

Yet from the perspective of church growth the hard truth is that worship services are the major place where people have their first contact with the local church. What we do there has a great deal to do with whether or not people return. And it will be hard for them to help us improve our motivations or for us to help them improve their motivations if the relationship does not continue.

Thus I have many specific suggestions to offer, but I make this particular offering with a certain amount of trepidation. I am not wanting to suggest that we should "perform" in the church, and I would be the first to agree that worship should not be evaluated by the same standards with which we evaluate events in the secular world. I hope that many of these suggestions can be taken in the spirit that they overcome obstacles which would otherwise be barriers to meaningful worship.

CONCEPT: When people come to the church to worship for the first or second time, SMALL THINGS COUNT.

In fact small things count so much that I've organized these points as a check-list which you can use to think about your own church. Some of these obviously apply to functions in the church in addition to worship services, but worship is the major focus here.

___ Are there signs from major streets which help people find the church? (See chapter eight.)

___ Is adequate parking available?

___ Is the parking clearly marked? If people are permitted to park in a department store lot, a school lot, or an office complex lot, are there signs which indicate that?

___ Is the church itself clearly marked? If there are other churches near you, and your building doesn't have a sign, people may well be confused – and go back home or go elsewhere! It does happen.

___ Are entrances to the church clearly marked? Can people tell which entrance to use for worship? In many churches, the big doors to the sanctuary are seldom used. Remember that visitors will tend to head for the largest doors.

___ Are greeters at the church entrances which will be used? People who are visiting always feel reassured if they are greeted quickly and given any needed information about the direction to the sanctuary (if there may be uncertainty), coat racks, restrooms, nursery, and so forth.

___ Are restrooms easy to find? Not everyone who needs to use the restroom will ask for directions. That isn't the most comfortable question to ask when you arrive. Major hallways in large church buildings should have signs which point the direction.

___ Are the restrooms clean and pleasant? If people are turned off by the restroom, they may very well be turned off by many other things. If the church restrooms have too much in common with filling station restooms, change is needed! What about paper toweling, toilet paper, soap?

___ If child care is provided, do the providers respond to newcomers with warmth and reassurance? Do they ask for information about the child and the name of the parents in the event there is an emergency? A warm greeting by the person or persons taking care of the children during worship goes a long way toward helping people feel good about the church.

___ Is the bulletin or the liturgy easy to follow? Think about it from the perspective of a newcomer.

___ If you say the Lord's prayer as a congregation, do you acknowledge being sinners or debtors? Is there a statement at that point in the bulletin or a word from the pulpit or lectern which lets people know which word to use? The bulletin can simply read: The Lord's Prayer (debtors)

___ Do ushers give clear directions on where to sit?

___ Are name tags available for visitors who want to wear them?

___ Is there a registration procedure so that names and addresses of visitors are obtained? Without that procedure, it's almost impossible to follow up on visitors.

___ Are offering instructions clear? People may be uncertain about whether or not to use envelopes that are in the pews. When ushers pass the plates, can people sitting near the end of a row readily tell whether to return the plate to an usher or pass it on?

___ If communion is served, are people informed clearly whether or not the Lord's table is open to those who are not members?

___ Are instructions for receiving communion clear?

___ Is a coffee/fellowship time available before or after each service of worship to give people opportunity to meet others and to visit informally?

___ Are several members in the habit of introducing themselves to others before and after worship services? Or will the visitor have to take all the initiative?

___ Is information about the church available in the form of a brochure or packet for those who would like to receive it?

___ Are announcements and "informal moments" in the worship service done with warmth and sensitivity to the fact that visitors may be present? Visitors usually respond well to statements of concern about persons who are hospitalized or in special need of prayer. Visitors can readily be turned off by lengthy announcements about meetings which only apply to a small number of persons.

___ If visitors are introduced, is it done graciously and without making them feel self-conscious?

___ Are the pastor and worship leaders well prepared? Do they help the service flow smoothly?

___ Is it easy to tell when to sit or stand during the service? Asterisks in the bulletin can help and can keep the worship leader from repeatedly saying "please stand" or "you may be seated." There are times, however, when a hand motion from a worship leader is helpful.

___ Are words provided in the bulletin or liturgy for any responses or songs (like the doxology) which may be familiar to members but will not necessarily be to nonmembers?

___ Does your sanctuary or place of worship show that the members care about its maintenance? A sanctuary does not have to be expensive or elaborate, but peeling paint and old bulletins in the pew racks do not say good things about respect for the place of worship.

___ Is hearing assistance available for any who have a problem? Is this information clearly provided in the bulletin, and are the ushers prepared to offer assistance?

___ Are accoustics and the microphone system (if you have a microphone system) reasonably good? Some churches have horrible accoustics made worse by an inadequate microphone/speaker system. One may not have to have a hearing impairment to have difficulty following the worship service. Spend what it takes to deal with that kind of problem.

___ Are children evident during the service? Children's sermons are not a requirement, but it's always good for children to be acknowledged during the service and for it to be clear that they are welcome in the sanctuary. Child care for the very young may be appropriate, but parents also need to feel that their children will be welcome at worship.

___ Do worship leaders avoid using too much "family" talk when referring to the church's program? Remember that a large percentage of those who come to worship are no part of a "nuclear family" with mother, father, and 2.2 children. Many couples, singles, and single parents will come. Don't use language which makes these people feel that the church is only concerned about families.

___ Do the prayers and meditations recognize that some persons will be present who are dealing with great pain and frustration in their lives?

___ Is the sermon or homily well organized and easy to follow? If not, then more time in preparation and more training may be appropriate.

Is the music which is performed appropriate to the abilities of the musicians? God may be equally praised by bad music as much as by good music, but human ears judge differently.

CONCEPT: Add worship services when appropriate; don't reduce the number of options available.

Many parishes are frustrated because of offering several worship services, each of which fails to fill much of the sanctuary. Active members often think "If we just had one big service, then the whole sanctuary could be full." In theory, right. In practice, wrong, wrong, wrong, wrong, wrong. And I emphasize this point because it is a strategic error made in many churches.

When you reduce the number of options available in your church (for worship services or almost anything else), you reduce participation. People quickly become accustomed to worshipping at a particular time. They don't want that time changed. They may even verbalize that they would be willing to come at a different time and then fail to do so when the change actually comes. It's not a matter of their being dishonest; it's a matter of the pervasiveness of habit and routine on the decisions which we make.

On the other hand, increasing options almost always helps nurture growth in attendance and membership. Some people will choose a church because of the Sunday morning schedule (and sometimes also the weekend and weekday schedule).

That doesn't mean you should automatically start adding worship services to increase your attendance and membership. It does mean that your evaluation of church program should include a careful look at the attendance patterns of members. You may also wish to get some data by talking with prospective members about what they like and dislike concerning your present schedule. Would people with small children find it easier to come if worship was available at 11 a. m.in addition to the 9 A. M. time? Are there enough people who are routinely gone on Sunday that you should have worship available on another day of the week? What benefits would you have from an early morning chapel service?

STARTING NEW GROUPS

*For though by this time you ought to be teachers, you need
some one to teach you again the first principles of God's word.
You need milk, not solid food; for every one who lives on milk
is unskilled in the word of righteousness, for he is a child. But
solid food is for the mature, for those who have their faculties
trained by practice to distinguish good from evil.*
Hebrews 5: 12-14

The fifth chapter of Hebrews sounds harsh in its view of those who
are not yet mature in the faith. Yet that chapter also embodies an
important truth about the life of the church–we are all at different
stages in our growth and represent a variety of life situations.

Parish programming needs to reflect the diversity of needs and
interests which characterize both current and prospective members.
A careful analysis of present programs against the needs of church
and community often leads parishes to add program opportunities. In
fact the addition of classes and groups can be one of the most
effective ways to stimulate significant parish growth (both by reaching
more nonmembers and by increasing the activity of present
members).

**CONCEPT: Most classes and groups have an upper limit on the
number of members who can be incorporated without some losses
in the percentage who remain active in the group.**

When people share in Bible study classes, prayer groups, women's
groups, youth groups, committees, boards, and task forces of the local
church, they place high importance on their identification with the
group and the value which they perceive themselves having to the
group. If one feels that his or her contributions to the group are
important and groups activities are enjoyable, that person will stay
active in the group.

A sense of "belonging," however, becomes hard to maintain when
a group reaches a certain size:

• Some small groups in which people share their most intimate
concerns and feelings may not function well with more than five
or six people. The introduction of more people raises the level of
anxiety over confidentiality being maintained.

• Many discussion and sharing groups find that with more than ten to twelve members, participants begin to drop out or to come less frequently.

• Traditional religious education classes and youth groups generally experience loss of activity by the time twenty to twenty-five members are part of the group. Additional teachers or counselors working with the group may increase the upper level, but it's unusual to find continuing church school classes and youth groups with an average attendance above twenty-five, regardless of the stated "membership" of the group.

• Classes which expect much of the session to be conducted by lecture and social groups which have carefully organized activities may actually continue to grow to a hundred members if leadership is strong. A few churches can point to even larger groups, but in most instances the percentage of persons coming each week will have tapered off by the time the group hit forty or fifty people. The fact that the group keeps growing doesn't necessarily mean that the percentage of members who remain active stays at the same level.

Thus new classes and groups often provide opportunities for growth which simply will not occur in continuing groups. When thinking about new classes or groups, always give consideration to present groups which seem to be near the maximum number that can be meaningfully involved.

CONCEPT: If persons agree before a new group has been formed that they would enjoy participation in such a group, the probability that they will participate if the group is formed runs around 30 percent for prospective members and 44 percent for present members. If those persons strongly want such a group, the percentage can rise to 72 percent.

When you talk with members and nonmembers about new groups or classes which would benefit your church, you have a rare and excellent opportunity to gain their interest and activity. People like to be asked their opinion, and they generally are enthusiastic when a new program or group is formed in response to their particular needs.

And this can hold true for a wide range of groups. Think about some of the following possibilities in relation to your church and community:

• A new Bible study group for youth
• A study group for young singles
• A support group for single parents
• A support group for persons who have had a husband, wife, or child die in the past year
• A group for young couples who don't have children
• A group for parents to talk about sex education and their teenagers
• An early morning men's prayer group
• A young singles group that meets for wine and cheese weekly (The wine is not workable in some denominational traditions!)
• A social group for young adults
• A church bowling league
• A group focusing on service projects to the poor
• An Easter season study group for those with children in the church's day care or nursery program
• A series of sessions on choosing a vocation for persons just graduating from college
• A series of sessions on self-confidence and job hunting for persons in a community with high unemployment
• A group for persons who want to learn sign language
• A group which goes to a movie once a week and then meets to discuss the film in relationship to the Christian faith and daily life
• A group for young parents to talk about child raising
• A group of retired persons who eat out together once a week
• A group which meets at the church and then goes calling on persons who are confined to their homes
• A group which deals with local hunger needs
• A group which studies mission opportunities

And the list can continue! When you match church programs with the interests and concerns of members or prospective members, you have the potential for involving many new persons.

CONCEPT: Most nonmembers of an existing class or group find attending the first several times an awkward experience; new classes and groups are not as threatening to persons who haven't been active in the parish.

Think of yourself as an inactive person in your church.
What's involved in coming to a class or group the first time if you have never been there before? You probably will have to introduce yourself. You may feel a need to say why you haven't come before.

You have a vague uneasiness because others in the group are already comfortable with each other. You have hesitancy about how people will react to your ideas and opinions.

Coming to a brand new class or group doesn't automatically remove all those barriers. Yet in a new class or group, everyone is in the same situation. A prospective member or a previously inactive member doesn't "stand out" so much from those who have been active in the church for years.

CONCEPT: Simply offering periodic options in continuing classes and groups doesn't solve the problem.

Many people feel that continuing adult classes and youth groups, for example, can provide a variety of topics for discussion. A schedule of topics can be published a quarter or a year at a time. That leaves people free to come and go from class sessions based on whether or not current topics meet their individual needs.

But that situation doesn't solve the problem for those who haven't been attending the class or group before. They will still feel the same awkwardness in coming for the first few times. And when the particular topic has been completed, persons who came just for that topic may displease regular group members by not coming any more. New classes and groups avoid these problems. The new classes and groups can be short term (4, 6, 8, or 10 weeks, for example) or continuing.

GUIDELINES FOR NEW CLASSES AND GROUPS

Whether you are starting a new long-term or short-term class or group, just announcing the opportunity in the parish bulletin or newsletter will not guarantee a successful beginning. Careful preparation makes all the difference. The guidelines below should be meticulously followed when starting a new group. These guidelines are not listed in any particular order – some will overlap, and all are important:

1. Be sure there really is interest in the group you are offering. New groups should be formed on the basis of established need. You may confirm such a need through:

- Requests from individuals in the church.
- Requests from a committee or task force (such as a youth

council, education board,....).
- Visits in the homes of members and prospective members.
- Surveys of members and prospective members.

If requests have come from only one or two persons, you generally want to do some informal visiting or surveying to confirm that such a need exists. Otherwise you may invest substantial energy in the promotion of a group that has an inadequate support base.

Remember as well that the lack of requests for a group doesn't mean that the need doesn't exist. That's why the careful examination of your parish membership and community recommended earlier in this chapter is so important. The point here is that once you think a need exists, you want to confirm that through a survey, visits, or the involvement of a board or committee.

2. Recruit specific persons for the group.

Contact, by phone or personal visit, persons you know should have an interest in the group. You may often find that this step and the first step are conducted at essentially the same time. You may have to begin some recruitment before you can be completely sure that the need is legitimate. The ideal, however, is to feel reasonably confident about the need through surveys and informal visiting before beginning strong recruitment efforts. You don't want to "hard sell" someone on a group that won't get off the ground!

3. Determine the minimum number necessary to begin the group and also the maximum the group can accommodate.

The maximum will depend on the subject and available leadership. A class that is primarily "lecture" or "presentation" in nature and that will use several "buzz groups" or "discussion groups" may be able to be very large. Some caring, sharing groups may need to be very small. As a rule of thumb, it's hard to maintain strong individual member identification with a group when more than twenty or twenty-five persons are involved. Many groups will reach an average attendance of twenty to twenty-five and not go beyond that size in regular attendance – even though the group itself may add more members.

The space available for the group will also make a big difference. Some physical settings place rigid restrictions on the size of a group.

4. Be certain you have good leadership before recruiting group members.

Ideally, the person or persons who will be teaching, advising, or coordinating the group should be part of the recruitment process. In some instance, you may be forming an adult group which will function with rotating leadership from the members themselves. Even in that situation, however, you need one or two people willing to assume the organizational responsibilities to get the group launched.

5. As you contact the first persons for the group, ask them who else they think would enjoy the opportunity.

They may suggest persons who are not connected with your church and may be willing to help recruit those persons. This kind of outreach is one of the most effective, and the beginning of a new class provides an ideal opportunity.

6. You should involve those who have a firm commitment to group membership in establishing the day and time for classes or meetings.

The day and time must be established early in the process. Most people will be unable to make a decision about the group without that information. If a regular meeting time is established with the first three or four interested persons, you will find others whose schedules will coincide. Try to avoid the trap of recruiting twelve people only to discover there is no time that will accommodate all twelve. If you do encounter persons who want to participate but whose schedules are in hopeless conflict, keep a record of them – perhaps they can be involved in a future group.

7. Determine the number of sessions needed (if the group is short-term), the resources needed, and the cost (if any) before recruiting people.

They have a right to know as much as possible about the group. If you are using a resource like this book, having copies available when you visit with persons about group membership will generally increase their interest in participation.

8. While you should not rely on bulletins, worship services, and newsletters to recruit the core membership for a new class or group, do take advantage of those means for additional publicity.
Although worship services can become so filled with announcements that they cease to be worshipful, a "minute speaker" about a new class

or group can often encourage participation. Include the names of leaders and perhaps also of some group members in the information which you share.

9. Be sure to include get-acquainted activities in the first few sessions, regardless of the topic for the group.

You will sometimes be fortunate enough to start a new group in which everyone truly knows everyone else. But if that is the case, you may be failing to include persons who have not been active in parish life before. Even if only one or two people do not know the others, it's important to take time to help that process.

10. Only begin one group or class at a time.

If you discover there are more interested persons than one group can accommodate, start another group later. Trying to do too much at once an result in frustration and failure.

Some churches which are especially well staffed with full time church workers or volunteers may actually find that they can begin several groups at once – especially in the fall when most parishes start their new program year. But churches well enough staffed to start more than one group at a time are the exception rather than the rule.

11. While some initial planning should precede the recruitment of group members, be sure to leave some areas for the group to decide.

For example, if you are starting a new Bible study group, you need to select a study resource, a meeting place, and a leader (or leaders) before much recruitment is done. Day and time also need to be identified if other than Sunday morning. The group itself, however, may well want to make decisions about how much time to spend on a particular topic, whether or not to have refreshments, and future directions for the group.

12. Be sure to keep track of attendance, and follow up quickly on any breaks in attendance.

Several sections of this book emphasize the importance of following up on breaks in attendance within a short period of time. The success of a new group can sometimes be greatly affected by how quickly you respond to breaks in attendance. If persons who said they were coming miss the first session, check with them right away. Don't wait until the next week to see if they come. They may be embarrassed for having missed the first session and automatically decide there is no point in coming.

During the first four weeks, you should check by phone on anyone who misses a session. If people are unhappy about something that happened in the group, you need to know that right away. If people simply broke the attendance pattern because of sickness, travel, work pressure, too little sleep the night before, or other
reasons, they need to know they were missed and are far more likely to return the next session.

The tone of your "follow up" should always be positive. Say something like: "We missed you. I thought you would like to know what we'll be doing next week . . . " Don't put the person on the spot to give a reason for the absence; do communicate your genuine interest in that person. If you start the conversation positively, you'll very likely find out if there was a specific problem which caused the absence. The"follow up" can be done by the group leader or by a designated member of the group.

14

SPIRITUAL GROWTH AND CHURCH GROWTH

*Not that I have already obtained this or am already perfect, but
I press on to make it my own, because Christ Jesus has made
me his own. Brethren, I do not consider that I have made it
my own; but one thing I do, forgetting what lies behind and
straining forward to what lies ahead, I press on toward the goal
for the prize of the upward call of God in Christ Jesus.*
Philippians 3: 12-14

Concern about spiritual growth should play a major part in our
individual and institutional thinking about church growth. While one
certainly recognizes that only a small percentage of the population
can in any way be considered highly spiritually committed, far larger
numbers of people, both inside and outside the church, actively
search for a deeper spiritual life. Considerable evidence supports that
view:

• Gallup polls consistently find that teenagers have high interest
in spiritual life retreats – and that's true of teens who are already
active in a local church and of teens who are not. Fifty-seven
percent of teenage girls and 46 percent of teenage boys say they
would like to participate in a spiritual life retreat.
• Churches around the country find that interest in religious
education classes, Bible study groups, and prayer groups has
increased.
• Over 90 percent of the population believe in God and identify
a religious preference. Yet a solid 30 percent of the population do
not hold membership in a local church. Many who are not church
members admit to desiring greater meaning and purpose in their
lives, yet they clearly have not been convinced that they can find
that meaning in a local church.
• Surveys consistently indicate that people have more confidence
in religion than in science as a source for solutions to the
problems of the world. And 56 percent of those surveyed by the
Gallup organization say they rely on God more than they did five
years ago.
• A large number of Americans say they want to come closer to

following the example of Christ in their own lives, yet no more than 10 percent feel they come close to that example.

• Among those who are highly spiritually committed, 6 percent describe themselves as "very happy" with their lives. That stands in marked contrast to only 30 percent of the uncommitted who feel that way.

• In a survey which I conducted of persons who do not belong to a local church, two-thirds indicated that they would readily join a church if they were convinced that church involvement would really help them grow closer to God and have a more meaningful life.

Churches which want to grow in membership and attendance need to take spiritual growth seriously. People inside and outside the church want to grow spiritually and want to find more meaning and purpose in their lives. Taking the need for spiritual growth seriously will benefit church growth in two major ways:

First, church members who are themselves growing spiritually will be far more ready to reach out to those who are not members of a local church. Serious Bible study, prayer, and discussion of the faith with others leads almost inevitably to a greater understanding of the importance of reaching out in Christ's name.

Second, spiritual growth opportunities attract persons who are not church members or who are currently inactive. In fact spiritual growth opportunities attract nonmembers more than almost any other form of church programming. Youth fellowship groups, couples' social groups, singles' fellowships, women's groups, men's groups, and music programs have important roles to play in outreach. But prayer groups, Bible study groups, religious education classes, and spiritual life retreats can be even more effective in reaching some people.

CONCEPT: The persons in your parish who volunteer to visit in the homes of members and nonmembers will be most effective if they share in a supportive group which includes Bible study and prayer.

We often send volunteers out to call in the homes of members (generally for the purpose of the "every member visitation," when financial support for the church is sought) with very little preparation or support. Yet most people would be more willing to do volunteer visiting and would find the experience significantly more satisfying if they received better training, spiritual preparation, and parish support.

Try having a group of persons (sometimes named the "Fishermen's Club" or the nonsexist "Fishers' Club" after the call of Jesus to Simon Peter and Andrew to become "fishers of men") meet on a weekly, bi-weekly, or monthly basis at the church. Begin with Bible study and prayer. Share visitation assignments and any information on procedures or approach to be used which will be helpful to the fishers. Then the group adjourns for people to do calling.

Even persons who choose to do most of their calling at times other than the night the support group meets will benefit from this kind of contact. Regular feedback about the impact done by the calling helps reinforce the practice, and people function much better when they have a supportive community for this kind of work. The Bible study and prayer play a major part because they help focus attention on the deeper motivations for the visitation program and provide a strengthening of the inner self which makes it easier to reach out.

Prayer groups in the church which may themselves not do calling can be asked to pray for those persons who are involved more actively in outreach on behalf of the church and to pray for those persons who are inactive members or nonmembers of the church. The building of a spiritual support base increases the confidence of those who do the visitation and provides more opportunities for Christ to work through us.

Obviously all the prayer in the world will not bring more members into the church unless people are willing to knock on doors and share the faith in their words and actions. But all the "busy work" in the world won't make a difference in the lives of others unless we are sufficiently open to the presence of Christ in our own lives.

CONCEPT: Growth in willingness to support the church financially almost always accompanies growth in the spiritual life.

Martin Luther observed centuries ago that three conversions are necessary:

- the heart
- the mind
- the purse!!

He was right. And conversion of the purse at times seems the most difficult task of all! In his insightful book Money, Sex, and Power, Richard Foster points out that discussion of money has almost become taboo. Many of us are more willing to talk about sex and death than about how we spend our money.

Talk about making money, of course, is another matter. We enjoy sharing ideas about how to make more money with others. But we don't want to share information about what we actually earn, what we actually have saved, or how we actually spend what we have.

And the church is often in the situation of getting the "leftovers" after we have taken care of other needs and desires. Current church giving stands at about 1.6 percent of annual income for the average Christian household. That stands in rather marked contrast to the 10 percent level which has traditionally been considered an appropriate base level for giving. If every person who belonged to a local church gave at the 10 percent level, over a hundred billion dollars a year would be generated for Christ's ministry.

It would, of course, be tragic for great increases to come in church support only to have that income spent on building bigger and more elaborate sanctuaries or in other ways just enhancing the church as an institution. Much of that money should go to spreading the Gospel in this country and abroad, and significant amounts of money should go the alleviation of world hunger by attacking root causes as well as providing immediate relief.

But increased financial support of the local church does have direct impact on our ability to reach out to others. Chapter nine on staffing for growth gave examples of three congregations which all needed more staff but felt they could not afford to hire more staff.

While there are many viable approaches to increasing levels of financial support for the local church, the very best motivation comes in helping members increasingly realize that all we have comes to us from God. We should use the financial resources we have been given in responsible ways that further Christ's work. Those persons who endeavor to grow spiritually almost inevitably find themselves more willing to share their financial resources. And they also find themselves happier in the process!

No other reasons for giving will make as much difference as basic recognition that our time, money, and talents all come to us from God and should be used for God's purposes. Those programmatic areas which need heavier financial support will be helped significantly when more people ar growing spiritually.

It's impossible to study the Bible seriously without dealing with financial issues. The Old Testament gave considerable attention to the use of material resources, and Christ's public ministry included many references to the use of wealth.

CONCEPT: Youth and young adults are far more interested in spiritual growth opportunities than in social opportunities as far as the church is concerned.

There was a period of time in youth and young adult ministry when church leaders felt that one had to start with games, parties, and other social events to gain the initial interest of youth and young adults. The parish hoped to attract youth to the church with enjoyable programs and in time introduce them to Bible study, prayer, and discussion of the spiritual life.

Some persons would argue that that approach never was the best one to use. Whether it was or not, the situation today clearly favors Bible study and spiritual growth opportunities over purely social events. Part of the reason for this simply rests in the incredible number of opportunities available to so many teenagers. If one turns the calendar back a hundred years to a time when more people lived in rural communities and transportation was not so readily available, the church appropriately becomes a social center for teens and young adult in a way that the church rarely is today. While we can lament the passage of that era if we wish, the truth is that youth and young adults have an enormous range of recreational options available to them today. Very few churches can successfully compete with movie theaters, restaurants, bowling alleys, the beach, bars, ski lodges, and automobiles in providing recreation. But churches can provide the opportunities for meaningful relationships with God and with one another which are missing from so many other settings.

Religious education classes, Bible study groups, and spiritual life retreats should constitute a major part of the outreach effort for most parishes. Given the interest of teens and young adults today, those kinds of opportunities will be positively received and very successful.

CONCEPT: The church should respond quickly when people are at life situations which raise spiritual questions in especially strong ways.

Think about the major crises and transitions which people experience in their lives. How many people could you name who have within the past year:

- Moved to a new community?
- Lost a job?
- Taken a new job?
- Started college?
- Graduated from college?
- Been seriously ill?

- Had a close friend seriously ill?
- Had a family member seriously ill?
- Suffered the death of a close friend?
- Suffered the death of a family member?
- Gone through a divorce?
- Suffered the breakup of a dating relationship?
- Suffered the breakup of a major friendship?
- Had a time of serious depression?
- Had a close friend going through serious depression?
- Had a family member going through serious depression?
- Attempted suicide?
- Had a close friend attempt suicide?
- Had a family member attempt suicide?

When people go through those kinds of experiences, they inevitably face many questions about the meaning and purpose of life. Questions about God, about relationships with other people, and about one's own growth as a person are all spiritual questions. The church needs to be quick to reach out to people who have had difficult experiences. Members who have their own lives centered on Christ find it easier to recognize when those around them are in need of help.

15

CHRISTIAN EDUCATION AND CHURCH GROWTH

*Every one then who hears these words of mine and does them
will be like a wise man who built his house upon the rock; and
the rain fell, and the floods came, and the winds blew and beat
upon that house, but it did not fall, because it had been
founded on the rock.*

Matthew 7:24-25

Christian education includes all the classes and groups in the parish
which serve a primary function of nurturing persons in the Christian
faith. Even though separate chapters on youth work and young adults
are included in this book, I see the parish Christian education
program incorporating those programs for the most part. C.C.D.
classes and religious education classes in parochial schools should
also be viewed as part of the church's Christian education program
I will not devote as much space to the discussion of parochial schools
in relationship to church growth because of limitations of space, but
I in no way underestimate the value which a good parochial school
program may offer to children and youth or the help it may give in
parish growth. People who are searching for an alternative to public
schools may well choose a particular church home because of the
quality of that church's parochial school program. I would also
suggest that the reputation of an outstanding youth program or
children "s program can have the same kind of impact.

Making a distinction between Christian education and spiritual
growth is a difficult task and probably not of immense importance. I
personally see Christian education as a broader concept,
incorporating the Bible study, prayer groups, and religious retreats
which are common to a spiritual growth emphasis. Christian
education may also include social organizations, religious education
classes for persons of all ages, service opportunities, and a wide range
of youth and adult programs. One could argue appropriately that all
Christian education focuses on spiritual growth and for that matter
that the entire program of the local church should focus on spiritual
growth.

Christian education at its best should be one of the primary evangelistic activities of the church. The dictum is old but true: "So goes the Sunday school, so goes the church." Declines in Protestant and Roman Catholic Christian education programs have almost always been followed by declines in church membership and average attendance. Increased participation in Christian education groups almost always results in membership and attendance gains for the church as a whole.

Most of the concepts to be covered in this chapter relate to the on-going Christian education program of the church—especially weekly classes for preschool, grade school, junior high, high school, and adult members, preparatory members, and nonmembers. These are generally held on Sunday morning but may include opportunities at other times.

CONCEPT: Many local church educational programs do not grow because they are understaffed. An insufficient number of teachers can cause decline in attendance. Adding teachers and leaders almost always make it easier to add students.

When a church wants to grow through its educational ministry, it seems logical to find creative ways to add students and then to add teachers as needed. It may be logical, but it generally doesn't work. Hard recruiting efforts only succeed in getting people to a class or group one time. Unless the teacher is well prepared for the group itself and prepared to follow up on absences, new students may not return. The agenda for the teachers or leaders of any group is enormous:

- Maintaining accurate records of those who are part of the group.
- Knowing all those who come to the class or group.
- Taking a personal interest in those who come.
- Being well prepared for class sessions.
- Following up on absences.
- Organizing efforts to reach out for new members.

Most classes and groups benefit greatly from having more than one person available for leadership. If only one person is available, then many of the above tasks simply will not get done.

CONCEPT: Take outreach especially seriously at the start of the new educational year for your parish.

Though the church fiscal year generally runs January 1 through December 31, the Christian education year more often runs from early September through the end of May. While summer programming is of great importance, promotion to the next class generally occurs in early September and coincides closely with the start of public school.

Because summer often is a "slack time" for church attendance and because people generally have special interest in the church in the fall, late August and September are often ideal times to reach out.

Over the past three years, I've had continuing confirmation that one of the best approaches involves the appointment of a committee or task force for each class with the purpose of adding members to the class. The committee or task force should generally include class members (except for preschool), parents, and the teachers. I would call the group a "task force" if it will only be active in preparation for the fall and a "committee" if it will function all year. That committee or task force should take the class roll and also brainstorm for the names of prospective students who have never been active in the church. Children and youth can think about people in their neighborhood and from school. Adults can think about work associates and neighborhood residents. You may be surprised at the number of names which you can generate of persons who are not involved in a religious educational program.

The teachers and the committee or task force should carry out a concentrated effort at contacting each student (already active, inactive, or prospective) – ideally with a home visit and certainly with a telephone call. Some churches find it helpful to arrange transportation for new students the first couples of Sundays. Bus ministries can provide this kind of help on a continuing basis.

When new students arrive, it is important for the teacher to take the initiative in sharing their names with the class and in helping class members get to know them.

Following the first attendance at a class or group, the teacher should:

1. Write or call to share appreciation for that person's attendance.

2. Notify the church office or pastor of the call having been made and of the address and phone of the new student.

3. Arrange for another student to call the newcomer and extend an invitation to share a soft drink or some other social event

during the week. Coffee or tea may be more appropriate for adults!

4. The teacher should be prepared to follow up the FIRST time there is a break in the attendance of the new student.

CONCEPT: You can't reach out to people if you don't know where they are or who they are.

Earlier chapters in this book have emphasized the importance of keeping track of names and addresses. Christian education class or group records are of enormous importance. Those records should include:

• Name, address, and phone for each student.
• Emergency information (in the event of illness if parents cannot be reached).
• Names of parents.
• The attendance record of students. The names of inactive students should only be dropped when you learn that a person has joined another church. Inactive persons should always be contacted at the start of a new Christian education program year. If that effort is unsuccessful, another contact should be made at least one more time during the year.

CONCEPT: Use greeters for your church school.

While churches often think about using greeters for worship services, many forget that the function is just as important for church school. In fact, greeters may be more important for the church school, because newcomers are often uncertain where to go for a particular class or group.

Also have an up to date directory and map of classrooms at each entrance to the church. You need this unless your church literally has only two or three rooms.

CONCEPT: Remember that appearance does count!

Encourage teachers to have classrooms neat and bulletin boards updated. Consider hosting an occasional "Clean It Out" evening to dispose of old materials and put up new materials. Encourage classes to hang banners, posters, and other results of class work.

If your church school hallways and rooms need painting or other refurbishing, by all means do so. Newcomers and continuing members will enjoy classes more in rooms that are attractive and that reflect the pride of the church.

CONCEPT: No other suggestions will have much meaning if teachers and leaders fail to be well prepared.

There are few short cuts to meaningful classes. The church needs leaders who are well prepared. And no matter how easy your curriculum materials are to use, preparation requires a certain amount of time. That's one of the reasons that I so strongly recommend a team approach to church school classes. The ability to share the preparation responsibility almost always results in better teaching.

CONCEPT: Use team teaching rather than rotating teaching to help with the work load for preschool, elementary, and youth classes.

I've had large numbers of people ask my opinion about the merits of rotating teachers. The systems vary:

Some classes change teachers once a quarter

Some classes change teachers once a month

Some classes have six people who keep rotating the teaching responsibility one Sunday at a time

While I appreciate the ease of teacher recruitment which such strategies make possible, my own observations of local churches continue to confirm that rotating teachers hurts the church school in the long run.

Teaching is not just a matter of presenting content which is then absorbed by those who come. Teaching involves relationships – between the teachers and the class and within the class. Much of the sense of Christ's presence which we gain through Christian education comes in those relationships. Rotation of the teaching responsibility makes it very difficult for meaningful relationships to be formed.

For preschoolers, the adult teachers are almost literally foster parents for the forty-five minute to two hour period of time the children are present. Elementary children and youth often form deep relationships with their adult teachers, and those teachers have tremendous opportunities for positive impact. But relationships suffer if leadership is changed every month or every quarter – let alone every week!

In team teaching, a group of persons shares the teaching responsibility. The team will most often be two or three people but with some larger classes may be as large as five or six. Sometimes those persons will decide to rotate the primary teaching responsibility from week to week, but the other members are also present to help with the class. Thus there are two or three adults with which class members can identify. While teachers will obviously be absent from time to time, there is an overall consistency in the people whom students find as their leaders. By having team teaching, the class responsibilities can be shared more readily, and it's easier for teachers to take a Sunday off when they need to be gone on vacation, to visit someone, or to take care of family concerns. Following up on absences, responding to new members, maintaining records, keeping the room attractive, and other tasks become much easier when more than one person helps with the teaching responsibility. This kind of approach virtually eliminates the need for a large number of substitute teachers. If there are three teachers on the team, the probability that all will be gone on the same day becomes very low.

Husbands and wives often make an excellent teaching team, and it's good for children to see couples working together in the church setting. Most churches have far more women than men helping with Christian education, which is a shame because men do an excellent job and children gain a great deal from identity with male teachers. If you use couples for team teaching and do not have another person working on the team, remember that you will have a greater need for substitutes since couples generally will miss at the same time.

CONCEPT: Awards for attendance can be positive reinforcement, but it is important not to place too much emphasis on them.

In earlier decades, attendance awards were frequently presented to Sunday School students in Protestant churches. The awards were generally in the form of a lapel pin. I had two friends who would go to Sunday School when they were physically ill in order to earn those pins. Before going into an extensive program of awards and recognition, it is important to recognize some potential pitfalls:

• Those receiving awards can develop an attitude of "I'm better than you are" which drives off less committed students.

• With some children, the attainment of the award becomes the purpose for attending educational activities. Thus the matter of growing in the Christian faith moves into secondary importance.
• An award program needs to be flexible enough to recognize that travel plans and sickness occasionally can keep even the most committed person from attending each week.

So an award program should be developed with clearly stated but flexible expectations. And it should be made clear that attendance alone is not the goal of a Christian education program. Further, both parents and teachers should be aware that words of personal appreciation and encouragement are usually better motivators than formal awards.

If you give awards, consider the possibility of presenting meaningful books, posters, or pictures as an alternative to pins. While pins are nice, many children and youth have limited occasions on which they can wear them.

CONCEPT: The most effective bus ministries are often developed in connection with Christian education programs.

Churches with the most effective bus ministry programs generally have those linked closely to their Christian education programs. By their nature, bus ministries tend to reach children, college students, and the elderly. These are persons for whom transportation to the church often stands as a barrier. In most communities, far more children will be reached than college students or the elderly.

All these persons are more likely to be drawn into church membership if actively involved in the Sunday school or church school rather than simply attending worship. Children obviously need the instruction and companionship of Christian education classes, but college students and the elderly benefit as well. Participation in these groups and careful follow-up by teachers can bring these people into full involvement.

Generally bus ministry schedules are established to bring people to the church both for church school classes and worship services. Churches which transport only for worship should consider a change in strategy.

Bus ministries, of course, can be valid even if they bring very few people into church membership. The transportation provision can be very important to the elderly and handicapped persons who already belong to the congregation. College students may have church membership in a home congregation and not be potential members, but they still need church involvement. Some churches establish a special "affiliate membership" for college students.

One of the chief concerns about bus ministries is that they so often bring children whose parents stay at home. The ideal, of course, is for the children to come to the church with their parents. hen that isn't happening, however, the bus ministry is one strategy for at least getting the children to the church. Those directly responsible for the bus ministry and teachers of the children can then work at strategies to involve the parents as well. Parents can be encouraged to attend for special programs in which their children participate, class parties, and other church events. Persons from the church may wish to call on those families to get acquainted with them and work toward fuller involvement.

Many churches with strong bus ministries are passionately convinced that it is crucial to reach the children even if the parents are never involved. We should be careful, though, not to give up on the parents. A carefully coordinated program can often lead parents into involvement through their children.

If your church is contemplating a bus ministry but not yet involved in one, find a nearby church with a successful bus program and visit with leaders about it. Find out how they organize, how they handle liability issues, and how expensive the program is. Be warned that bus ministries require significant expenditures of both dollars and volunteer hours. The information you gain will help you in making a decision about initiating a bus ministry for your church.

If you begin a bus ministry primarily as a form of outreach to children, consider the following factors in developing your program:

1. Bus drivers need to be highly committed persons with the appropriate driver's license and with a lot of warmth for people. Some churches staff each bus with a team – one person to focus on driving and the other to focus on contact with the passengers.

2. Bus drivers or the bus team often canvass neighborhoods on Saturday to see who would like to be picked up on Sunday. For a brand new bus ministry, it is crucial to begin in this way. The parents get to meet the driver and will always feel better about their children participating as a result of that contact. The driver or team can write down the name, address, phone, and an emergency contact for the child. It is critical to have that information.

3. Be sure that greeters are on hand at the church to direct bus passengers to classes and worship services. Young children need to

be taken to the classroom by an adult leader.

4. Help teachers develop special programs, parties, and other activities to which parents can be invited.

5. Have the bus driver or team, teachers, or other volunteers make return visits to parents in order to update them on the progress of their children and to encourage them to become more fully involved in the parish.

6. Establish a regular preventive maintenance schedule for the vans or buses used by your church.

7. Be sure that you have adequate liability insurance covering the drivers and the church.

8. Identify as many opportunities as possible for use of the vehicles so that you get good return on the church's investment. While Sunday morning transportation may be the major focus, the vehicles can also be used to transport people to senior citizens' meetings, to help the handicapped (if designed to accommodate persons with mobility problems), to transport youth for church activities, and for midweek children's programs and choir rehearsals. Be certain, however, that the volunteer drivers or teams if the buses will have extensive midweek use. Don't rotate drivers or teams on Sundays. Children riding the bus need the continuity of seeing the same driver each Sunday. Vacation replacements are necessary, but keep change to a minimum. Different drivers or teams for midweek activities will not pose the same problem as rotation on Sunday.

YOUR CHURCH SCHOOL PROGRAM AND FACILITIES

Use the checklist which follows to stimulate your own thinking about your church school or religious education program. While some of the items listed may not seem to affect growth in membership and attendance, they do affect quality – and the quality of your program ultimately has a great deal to do with the growth which you achieve. Try using this list with teachers and other educational leaders in your parish.

Our Facilities

____ We have an adequate number of classrooms to met our needs.

____ Our classrooms are large enough for the groups which
      currently meet in them.

____ Our classrooms are large enough to allow some growth in the
      size of most groups which meet in them.

____ We have an adequate number of classrooms to allow for some
      growth in number of classes or groups offered.

____ Our rooms are clean and attractive.

____ Our hallways are clean and attractive.

____ Our classrooms have furniture that's adequate and in good
      condition.

____ We have attractive and adequate rest room facilities for
      our church school.

____ We have a central source of supply for markers, newsprint
      and other teachings aids.

____ We purchase some audio-visuals ourselves.

____ We share in an arrangement which lets us rent or use audio-
      visuals in cooperation with other churches.

____ We have filmstrip projectors, cassette players, and record
      players in good condition for classroom use.

____ We have or can borrow motion picture projector(s) as needed.

____ We have purchased or are considering purchasing video
      player equipment to take advantage of new religious and
      secular video resources.

____ We have at least one computer available for use by our
      church school.

____ Posters, bulletin boards, and other display items in our
      classrooms are current and attractive.

Our Volunteer Staff

____ We have a nominating committee or other group responsible to see that adequate numbers of teachers and other educational leaders are recruited.

____ When someone is recruited for a leadership role in the church school, that person is provided with the needed training.

____ When someone is recruited for a leadership role in the church school, the expectations of the position are made clear.

____ When someone is recruited for a leadership role in the church school, the tenure for the position is made clear.

____ Our teachers and leaders know the procedure to use if they need materials or equipment which they do not have in their rooms.

____ We have a system which insures that each teacher or leader has a supervising teacher, counseling teacher, church school superintendent, age level coordinator, or other person who checks on a regular basis to see what assistance is needed.

____ We use team teaching in most of our classes. (Team teaching means having two, three, or more persons sharing the class responsibility.)

____ We provide periodic workshops to help our teachers and educational leaders.

____ We show appreciation to our teachers and educational leaders at morning worship at least once a year.

____ We have ways of reinforcing and encouraging teachers and educational leaders throughout the year.

____ We include many men as well as women on the teaching staff.

____ Our pastor and other leaders make it clear that teaching is an important responsibility, and our teachers are held in high respect.

____ We have an adequate number of substitute teachers available.

____ If a teacher is going to be absent on a particular Sunday, he or she knows who should be notified.

The Teaching Task

____ Our teachers are encouraged to use a variety of methods in working with classes, including

____ finger painting
____ poster making
____ collage making (gluing down words, pictures, string, etc.)
____ clay molding
____ writing stories
____ writing poetry
____ acting out Bible stories
____ role playing
____ quiz contests on the Bible
____ drama
____ crossword puzzles
____ talking about real life situations
____ filmstrips
____ movies
____ video tapes
____ computers
____ using buzz groups or discussion groups
____ doing pantomimes
____ completing sentences or doing multiple-choice exercises
____ using outside resource persons
____ having circular responses (going around the circle with each person sharing his or her opinion)
____ making mobiles
____ other craft projects
____ using puppets
____ having panel discussions
____ debating important issues
____ having field trips or other outings (visiting the sanctuary; visiting a funeral home; visiting a synagogue)

____ We have enough teachers for good discipline in all our classes.

_____ Our teachers know how to show their concern for students.

_____ Our teachers personally know each of their students.

_____ Our teachers do careful preparation for each session.

_____ Our teachers have been given enough help to know how to effectively use our church school curriculum.

Direct Attendance Concerns

_____ Our teachers or leaders maintain accurate and current class records.

_____ If a new student comes, that person is warmly welcomed and helped to meet others in the class or group.

_____ If a new student comes, that information gets shared with the pastor or the church office.

_____ When the pastor or church office lets us know about a new family with an interest in our church, those classes which have students of that age get in contact with that family.

_____ We give rewards or recognition to those who maintain regular attendance.

_____ If someone who has been coming stops coming, a contact by phone is made with that person within two or three weeks.

_____ If a phone contact doesn't bring someone back to regular attendance, a visit will be made to that home.

_____ We encourage class members to bring friends to class.

_____ We have exercises to help children, young people, and adults feel more comfortable talking about their faith with others.

16

REACHING MORE TEENAGERS

*Then I said,"Ah, Lord God! Behold, I do not know how to
speak for I am only a youth." But the Lord said to me, "Do not
say 'I am only a youth'; for to all to whom I send you shall go,
and whatever I command you, you shall speak. Be not afraid
of them, for I am with you to deliver you, says the Lord."*
                                                    Jeremiah 1:6-8

Jeremiah felt he was too young to carry God's message, but the
Lord clearly did not accept that argument. When we think about
teenagers, we often feel that we are talking about the church of the
future – the teens of today will be the church leaders of tomorrow.
But that attitude is a misconception. Young people can contribute a
great deal to the church today; and the more fully teens are involved
in our churches now, the more fully they will be involved as adults.

The exact boundaries for youth work in the local church depend to
some extent on public school organization in your community. Most
denominations think of junior highs as seventh and eighth graders
and of senior highs as ninth through twelfth graders. In some
communities, junior highs may include sixth graders and ninth
graders. Once a young person has finished high school, most churches
find it helpful to think of that person as a young adult even though he
or she may still be in the teen years.

**CONCEPT: You need to involve in youth ministry people who
genuinely love teenagers, for the relationships adult leaders form
with teenagers set the climate for your youth ministry.**

While relationships between teachers or leaders and students are
important at every age level, they are of special significance in work
with teenagers. (By "teenagers" throughout this chapter, I'll be
referring to junior high and senior high young people.) You need to
find adults who experience great satisfaction from contact with youth.

In most parishes, you'll find the best results if you recruit a group
of people for youth ministry. There are several reasons for this:

• The more adults involved, the greater the probability of there
being an adult with whom each teen will positively identify

• Having too much work and responsibility falling on only one or two people contributes to a very high rate of "youth worker burnout." The danger is real – the average tenure of a volunteer youth worker is shorter than for any other Christian education volunteer category.

• The group of adults can provide mutual support and be a source of continuing ideas to help each other.

Don't be fooled into thinking that only relatively young people can work well with teenagers. That's simply not so. Middle aged adults and senior citizens often make excellent youth workers. Young adults can also do an excellent job, but there is danger when you have youth workers who are too close in age to the teens for whom they are responsible. While they bring great enthusiasm to youth work, they may not bring the maturity and perspective that teens need. In making that statement, I'm also aware that some of the finest youth workers I've known were only nineteen or twenty years old. There simply are no hard and fast rules. You want to recruit people who are mature, who are comfortable expressing their own faith, and who like teenagers.

In recruiting volunteers, you also want to make it clear that one of your concerns as a church is to reach more teenagers. You want volunteers who share that desire. An inevitable tension often comes in youth work. If the leader of a youth class or group does a good job building closeness within the group, group members may become "closed" to the possibility of others joining the group. Thus one finds an ironic situation – the very success of the group ends up working against successfully adding new persons to the group. This same problem can be present with adults but is even more likely to be present with teenagers. There are two ways to deal with this situation:

1. Recognize that this will happen. If your church's youth programming proves attractive to teens, you may well have to add new groups. There's nothing wrong with that.

2. In work with the members of a class or group, be sure to focus on the outreach dimension of spiritual growth. Help teens understand that part of expressing our love for Christ includes reaching out to others with that love. Teens who are helped to understand the legitimate place of outreach in the spiritual life will become good advocates for Christ and the church. Groups which are closed to the involvement of others very often have focused more on interpersonal relationships than on Bible study and spiritual growth.

While interpersonal relationships are important and merit emphasis, spiritual growth also needs to be part of the program.

CONCEPT: Build a total youth program for your church which includes a balance of: (1) learning and spiritual growth experiences; (2) worship experiences; (3) recreation and social events; and (4) service opportunities.

Local church youth programs often end up heavy on only one or two of the four dimensions shared in this concept, but all four dimensions are important if your youth program is going to help young people in their own growth and if the program itself is going to grow numerically. The focus of youth programming in many churches comes in a Sunday evening youth group–generally one group for junior highs and another for senior highs. The most successful groups of that sort take seriously the need for balance. Some will plan schedules following a rotating plan something like this:

- 1st Sunday: Bible study or learning program
- 2nd Sunday: A service project for church or community
- 3rd Sunday: Bible study or learning program
- 4th Sunday: Party or recreation
- EVERY SUNDAY: Time for sharing concerns of group members and joining in prayer (worship)
- EVERY SUNDAY: Time for refreshments

While traditional Sunday evening youth groups generally work best with the kind of balance just described, you don't have to achieve that same balance in every youth program of your church. You want to be sure, however, that the total youth program offerings of your church provide a balance of experiences and opportunities. There's nothing wrong with having groups with focuses like these:

- A morning Bible study group
- A Wednesday afternoon bowling group
- A summer softball team
- A Good Samaritan group (that fixes up homes for the poor; does chores for shut-ins; performs volunteer work for the church.
- An evening spiritual growth group
- A choral group
- A group that discusses popular music (MTV!) and films (videos)

Remember that you want to have as wide a range of opportunities as your church size permits.

CONCEPT: Include spiritual life retreats in your program offerings.

The value of spiritual life retreats has already been discussed in this book. With 57 percent of teenage girls and 46 percent of teenage boys open to participation in these events, every church should have at least one a year and should make an intentional effort to reach inactive members and nonmembers for involvement in the retreat. This can prove the single most effective outreach for many parishes.

The advantage of a retreat is that it provides a limited commitment (for those who aren't sure how much involvement they want to have with the church) that is sufficiently long to let the young people and the youth workers build positive relationships with one another. Many denominations have materials which are appropriate for use in these retreats.

Have scholarships available for the spiritual life retreat either through funds earned by the young people themselves or through another organization in your church. Have young people publicize the retreat to their friends and invite them to participate.

CONCEPT: Do careful evaluation of the membership preparation process in your church; you want to reach as many young people as possible at this time and to form a foundation which will keep them active in the years ahead.

While denominational traditions vary, most churches offer some kind of special membership instruction or preparation between the fifth and the ninth grades. That instruction is often, but not always, offered by the pastor. Following the period of instruction, young people have the opportunity to become formal members of the church.

This provides an ideal opportunity for outreach. Many parents who normally show little concern about the activity of their children in the church do want their offspring to become members and will encourage their attendance at these classes. Go through Sunday School class rolls, youth group records, and member records to find all those of the appropriate age for membership preparation. Have young people themselves identify friends who do not have a church home and who might be approached about these classes.

But you also want to be sure the class provides the kind of

experiences that will keep young people actively involved. Try doing an informal survey of those who have participated in membership preparation classes over the last three or four years. Find out what was helpful and what was not helpful. Ask them in what ways the class might have helped them grow closer to God and to each other.

CONCEPT: Have intensive follow up on youth members after they have been formally confirmed into the church.

The pattern is all too common:

- 20 youth are confirmed as eighth graders in 1987
- In 1988, only 15 of those teens are active
- In 1989, only 11 of those teens are active
- In 1990, only 8 of those teens are active
- In 1991, only 5 of those teens are active

The rest have become inactive church members someplace along the way between confirmation and high school graduation. While the exact numbers and percentages vary from church to church, the trend is tragically familiar.

This doesn't mean that the young people or their parents are insincere at the time of membership preparation or when confirmed into the church. It simply reflects the reality that the high school years are ones of high pressure on young people with many individuals, projects, and groups competing for their time. Unless those of us in the church are very intentional at staying in touch with teens and offering programs that are meaningful, we may find them disappearing from regular activity.

Have careful follow up on those who change their activity pattern. Offer new groups and opportunities when appropriate. Learn to listen to the needs of teenagers. When church programs respond to those needs and help deepen the spiritual life, youth keep coming.

Also remember that not all teens can be involved in every program of the church. Some teens may choose only to participate in worship services. While teenagers obviously need to keep learning, be sure your encouragement is positive rather than negative. Going to worship alone isn't as good as being involved in a class or group in addition to worship – but it's a lot better than not participating in the church! All of us as adults have to make choices about the church programs in which we will be involved; many young people must do the same. The point for the church is to keep them involved in meaningful ways and to encourage them to take part in spiritual growth opportunities as often as possible.

Have a group or committee in your church which is responsible for your overall program of youth outreach. This may be a "Youth Council" or simply a task force of your education committee. It is important to have a group looking at your total youth program and recommending changes and new programs where appropriate.

CONCEPT: Be sure that young people themselves are actively involved in planning your church's youth ministry.

Teens need to be involved in planning activities within individual classes and groups, and they need to be involved in shaping your church's total youth program. Be certain you have teenagers on your youth council, education committee, and any other groups which are concerned with young people. The young people themselves have a great deal to contribute and will respond far more positively when they've been involved in the planning process.

CONCEPT: If your church can afford part-time or full-time staff additions, consider doing more in the area of youth work.

If a year round employed youth worker is too great a cost for your parish, consider the possibility of hiring a college student in the summer for some special youth programming. (Remember the comments on volunteers earlier in this chapter; you want to employ someone who is sufficiently mature to be a good example to teens and to be comfortable sharing his or her faith.) If your church has large numbers of inactive teens, you can benefit greatly from having a college student spend the summer calling on all the teens in your parish. Find out why those who are inactive have chosen to be that way; find out what new programs or changes in existing programs would be helpful; and encourage the young people to become involved.

CONCEPT: Be certain that teens are given help in learning how to share their faith with others.

Sharing one's faith is not an easy task for many people (including adults as well as teenagers). We need to help teens become more comfortable sharing their faith and reaching out to others. When teens have been given that help, they are far more willing to try and get others to participate in church programs. The "Guidelines for Youth Witnessing" which follow can be used as a basis for discussion in youth classes and groups.

GUIDELINES FOR YOUTH WITNESSING

Many young people are not comfortable talking about their faith outside of the church setting, and they need encouragement in order to do so. Other young people, though armed with the best intentions, may give non-Christians or nonmembers just enough dose of slightly distorted Christianity to forever inoculate them against the real thing. It is very important to be specific in instructing others to witness. The following Do's and Don'ts are helpful guidelines for youth witnessing. Use them as a basis for discussion in youth groups or classes. You may also find them helpful with adult groups.

1. DO consciously identify friends who are not members of a church and give no indication of professing the Christian faith. Almost everyone knows some people in this category. Also identify friends who seem to share the Christian faith but who do not belong to a church.

2. DON'T attempt to "win" those who are already a part of another church or religious community. While the approaches of Lutherans, Roman Catholics, United Presbyterians, American Baptists, Church of the Brethren, Pentecostals, Mennonites, and United Methodists may vary, they all profess faith in Jesus Christ as Lord. The churches to which they belong have the primary responsibility for their Christian development. In Biblical times, the process of taking members away from another religious community was called proselyting. This approach may help build a local church, but it does not build the kingdom of God. Your energy is better spent on the inactives in your own church or on those with no church connection.

3. DO share what your relationship with Christ means to you at appropriate times in normal conversation. If Christ is the center of your life, then many of your decisions should be influenced or determined by your faith. Let others know when you feel that Christ has helped you make a difficult decision or cope with a significant problem.

4. DON'T be caught with inconsistency between what you say and what you do. If you smoke, drink to excess, cheat, manipulate others, and do other things which are generally seen as inconsistent with being a Christian, people will have trouble believing your witness for Christ. This does not mean that you adopt a lifestyle which is

sickeningly sweet like a mix of honey, maple syrup, brown sugar, and pop. It does mean that your faith in Christ should be influencing your daily habits and decisions. Others cannot help evaluating your faith by your behavior.

5. Do build friendships with persons whom you would like to win for the Christian faith. If you come on strongly about Christ to people whom you do not know well, they will assume (perhaps correctly) that your only interest in them is to gain another scalp for evangelism. Your words about Christ will have the most meaning when addressed to persons who know that you like them and care about them.

6. DON'T drop your friendship with another person when that person accepts Christ and becomes active in the church. If you formed a friendship with that person for the sake of conversion, your losing interest in that friendship will hurt him or her deeply.

You should be careful in building a relationship with a person who does not belong to a church or who does not believe in Christ that you do not appear to be offering a deeper friendship that you are willing to continue. Be sincere in your relationships, and express feelings of genuine concern and appreciation. Do not act like you want another person as your best friend unless you really do.

This caution is particularly important in relationships with the opposite sex. It is cruel to date someone for the ulterior motive of converting that person.

7. DO follow Christ's example in caring about other people. Be alert to persons who are particularly lonely or isolated because of physical handicaps, low incomes, or ethnic background. You should reach out in concern and friendship. As you reach out to such persons, you will find that your own life has been enriched.

You may want to do some self-assessment. Make a list of your closest friends; others whom you consider good friends; and persons whom you like but with whom you do not spend much time. Are physically handicapped persons on that list? What about persons whose families have low incomes? What about persons of different races? You may be losing a great deal personally by not having friends from those categories.

8. DON'T act in a condescending way toward non-Christians or nonmembers of a church. Being a Christian does not make anyone better than other people. All people are children of God and as such

are of great worth in the sight of God. Attitudes of arrogance and superiority are inconsistent with the Christian faith, and you will do little to advance the kingdom of God with such an attitude.

9. DO ask others to join you at church activities which are open to nonmembers. Many people have developed faith in Christ through contact with a good youth group. Activities like retreats, lock-ins, films, and parties may be especially good for those who feel threatened about church contact.

Also remain sensitive to the fact that many people who don't belong to a church nevertheless have strong beliefs about God and want to develop a deeper relationship with Jesus Christ. Those persons may actually be more interested in invitations to Bible study, church school class, or a prayer group than to a purely social event. Spiritual life retreats tend to be popular with most young people, whether those young people have been active in the church or not.

10. DON'T personally invite large numbers of people at the same time. If you invite a person to attend a church activity with you, then you should arrange transportation for that person, stay with him or her during the activity, and provide introductions to other people. You probably can only do this effectively for one person at a time. If you identify a second person who should be invited to a church activity, it is best to ask another member of your group to invite that person.

11. DO practice talking about your faith with others. Practice completing sentences like these:

- I am a Christian because . . .
- I feel certain of God's presence when . . .
- I want others to know about God because . . .
- Worshipping in church helps me by . . .
- My youth group helps me by . . .
- I feel closest to God when . . .
- My faith in Christ has helped me . . .
- I think prayer helps me . . .
- Studying the Bible means a lot to me because . . .

Another approach is to pair with another person who also wants to become more comfortable witnessing to others. Take turns role playing the part of a non-Christian, nonmember of a church, or inactive church member. The other should interpret the Christian faith or the merits of church involvement to that person. Then reverse roles. Share reflections on the experience. Sentences such as the following are possible discussion openers:

* My church youth group is going on a retreat this weekend. I'd like to have you come as my guest . . .
* I know that some of the Jesus saves types have really turned you off to the church. I don't blame you, but I hope you don't think all Christian people are like that . . .
* I've not talked a lot about it but my faith in God has really helped me get through some hard times this year. I'd like to share my experience with you, if you'd be interested in hearing about it ...
* I feel uncomfortable trying to tell someone else about my faith in God. I'd like to talk with you about it . . .
* My church youth group is one of the most enjoyable groups of people that I've known. Would you be interested in joining the group or at least in visiting it? . . .
* I don't know why some things are so hard to talk about. My parents avoid talking about sex. Lots of people don't want to talk about suicide or death. And then sometimes I find myself not feeling comfortable talking about the church . . .

12. DON'T use religious cliches. Most people who aren't active in church (and many who are) have grown tired of phrases like:

* Are you saved?
* Have you accepted Christ?
* What would happen if you died tomorrow?

Those phrases have been badly overworked and turn off many people. That doesn't mean there is anything wrong with people who use the phrases and certainly not that there is anything wrong with the ideas behind the phrases. But you'll have more success witnessing to most people if you avoid overworked phrases and terms.

13. DO seek answers to your own questions about God, the Bible, and the church. You will be better able to interpret your faith if you are growing in your own knowledge and understanding. Seek help from your minister, group advisor, teacher, or parents.

14. DON'T feel that you must have all the answers before sharing your faith with others. No one has all the answers! Committed Christian people have strong differences of opinion on such subjects

as: the literal account of creation, the virgin birth, whether non-Christians will be saved, the nature of heaven and hell, and the nature of miracles. If you wait until you have all the answers, you will end up sharing your faith with no one! If you are convinced of the reality of God and of His love for you and others, you are ready to share your faith with others. Keep growing, keep learning, and keep caring about other people as Christ has cared for you.

15. DO share with God in prayer your concerns about witnessing to others. Seek God's guidance in identifying persons who would benefit from hearing your witness or receiving an invitation to the church. Seek God's help in approaching people in the best way. Seek God's patience and understanding when you find that some people do not respond as you hoped they would. Give God thanks for the good experiences you have reaching out to others.

16. DON'T delay starting to talk more with others about your faith and about what the church means to you. You'll never reach an ideal time to start sharing the faith. TODAY would be a good day to start.

The preceding guidelines are based on those in The Youth Workers' Handbook *by Steve Clapp and Jerry O. Cook.*

17

Reaching More Young Adults

> *Jesus, when he began his ministry, was about*
> *thirty years of age . . .*
>
> Luke 3:23a

Defining "young adults" is itself a difficult task. Through most of recorded history, societies have tended to recognize just two stages in development: childhood and adulthood. In more recent decades, the categories of "youth" and "young adults" have begun to emerge. As the passage from Luke indicates, Christ was about thirty years of age when He began His public ministry. In New Testament times, thirty was not an especially young age. People died at an early age, and women often became mothers as young as fifteen or sixteen.

With the passage of time, however, the age at which persons have been expected to assume adult responsibilities has steadily increased. The growing necessity of people completing high school lengthened the time in which children were financially and emotionally dependent on their parents. Society increasingly recognized that teenagers were not really "children," but calling them adults seemed wrong when they had so much continued dependency and when their full emotional development was not complete. Thus we gained "youth" as a meaningful category in thinking about development.

But you and I are well aware that a high school education alone doesn't prepare people for life in the way which it once did. Now the period of semi-dependency continues long enough to let people complete college, nurse's training, armed forces instruction, trade school, or some other kind of background related to vocational choice. And the years following the completion of that training have also been characterized by shifts in vocation and by sorting out one's major directions in life. We have also increasingly recognized distinctions in values and attitudes between younger adults and middle aged adults.

Thus many social scientists and institutions, including the church, have begun to talk about "young adults" as a category between "youth" and "middle aged adults." Many denominations now define this category as beginning at nineteen years of age (or immediately following graduation from high school) and continuing through thirty-five years of age, whether married or single. While there are many arbitrary aspects to this category which make it hard to be as precise as we can with "children" or "youth," most of us recognize that it exists as a meaningful distinction.

And those of us in the church can look at young adults in another way—these are the persons who most of our churches have had the most difficulty holding in active membership during the last twenty years. During some earlier periods of time, some churches anticipated that many people would become inactive in church by the time of high school graduation; but those same churches anticipated that the individuals would return to activity almost automatically when they got married and began having children.

Whether or not the transition from inactivity to activity ever happened as automatically or neatly as we like to think in retrospect the harsh reality is that it hasn't been happening well for the last several years. Part of the reason is that more persons in the young adult years are waiting longer to get married, and a greater percentage than in the past are deciding not to get married at all. But even those who do get married have been slower to return to the church.

The very latest indications are that the tide is starting to turn. Young adults are being pulled toward the church again. Unfortunately, they are not being pulled toward the church at the speed with which they left the church. But the significant interest of young adults in religious issues and the greater openness toward the church which is present today means that we have some excellent opportunities.

CONCEPT: The local church must recognize the diversity represented by young adults today. No individual program will reach all the young adults in any parish.

Think for a few minutes about the life situations of people in your church or community who fall into the nineteen to thirty-five years of age category. You'll probably identify:

- single students in college
- married students in college
- people in the armed forces
- people in nurse's training
- people in auto training

- persons working in factory jobs
- persons working in professional jobs
- singles well into their late twenties or early thirties
  who appear willing to stay single for life
- married persons who both work
- married persons who have children and who both work outside
  the home
- married persons who have children and only one spouse works
  outside the home
- single parents who work

You can think of persons who meet all of the above descriptions and can probably identify other young adults who wouldn't fit in any of the categories just given. Your parish program for young adults must recognize that kind of diversity. A twenty-four year old single female in graduate school may have no more in common with the thirty year old couple who both work and have two children than with a high school student or a middle aged person. The same program is not likely to equally serve all young adults.

This doesn't mean that your church can't have successful young adult ministries unless you have enough members and resources to offer six or seven different young adult groups. After all, the church as a whole is even more diverse than the young adult category, and we bring all that diversity together successfully for worship each week. Recognizing the diversity, however, will keep us from making some errors in our programming assumptions.

CONCEPT: Bible study can provide some of the best opportunities for involving young adults, regardless of the size of your church.

Bible study provides common ground for most young adults. The Bible speaks clearly to many of the life issues that are important to young adults, and study of the Scriptures with others does much to enhance the understanding of each person. Bible study and spiritual growth opportunities are your best direction for work with many young adults. Intergenerational Bible study groups may also be very successful.

You should, of course, also be alert to special interest groups which can respond to the needs of young adults:

- Social groups for singles
- Couples groups
- Support groups for young parents

- Support groups for single parents
- Groups organized to talk about vocational decisions
  and directions
- Marriage preparation groups
- Seminars on young adult dating and sexuality
- Marriage enrichment groups
- Support groups for armed forces personnel
- Fellowship groups for college students
- Seminars in career assessment and planning

CONCEPT: Young adults need to be involved in all phases of the church's decision making.

While special groups that appeal to young adults and speak meaningfully to their needs are important, this doesn't mean that young adults should be kept in a category to themselves. In fact one of the chief barriers to many churches reaching more young adults is the failure of the church to involve them fully in decision making. The young adult perspective is particularly needed in selecting new church staff members, in deciding how to spend church funds, in making decisions about the use of church property, and in determining the kinds of study and enrichment opportunities to be offered by the church.

If you don't have enough young adults available to place them on each decision making group in the church, then be sure to include them on the major board or council for your parish. Their perspective will keep your decisions sensitive to the needs of this category of persons.

CONCEPT: Don't propose new programs and assume that young adults will begin to respond to the church; reach out to young adults and involve them in designing those programs.

With young adults, as with virtually any other group in the parish, church leaders need to take the initiative in reaching out. Most parishes have more young adults with at least fringe contact with the church than is often realized. Start checking:

- The membership and baptismal rolls of the church for
  persons in the young adult years

- Old church school and youth group records for names of
  people who would now be young adults but who dropped

out of church activity

- With active members of the church for the names of young adults with whom they are acquainted

- With college and armed forces administrators about young adults in your community

- With newcomer organizations and other sources of information about people moving into the community

You may be pleasantly surprised at the number of names you can identify. If the church takes initiative in reaching out to these young adults, you will also be pleasantly surprised at how positive the response of many of them will be.

CONCEPT: Churches which involve significant numbers of young adults may have to deal with some values conflicts with older members of the congregation.

While young adults definitely are more conservative in their values and standards in the late nineteen eighties than in the middle seventies, differences still exist between the perspective of young adults and of older church members. Young adults who have chosen to be inactive in the church are especially more likely than older adults who are active in the church to:

- believe that sexual activity before marriage is all right when both parties consent

- feel that couples should consider living together before marriage (or at least feel there is nothing wrong with their doing so)

- be strongly in favor of nuclear disarmament

- feel that divorce is satisfactory when no other solution can be found

- feel that abortion is the best of bad options for some people

- feel that parenting should be shared equally by

husband and wife and that the wife should continue
her career even when the child is small if that is
the wife's desire

- feel that smoking and drinking are individual decisions
  in which the church should not interfere

- feel that a person can be a good Christian without being
  active in a local church (even if they themselves choose
  to be active)

- feel that ethnic background and religious persuasion
  should not limit one's choice of husband or wife

The church can live with this kind of diversity, but the reality needs
to be recognized. Many young adults do stay away from the church
because they anticipate that they will be criticized (publicly or
privately) if they are honest in the church about their values and
attitudes. Churches characterized by high respect for diversity of
opinion in the Christian community will be the most likely to involve
large numbers of young adults.

CHILD CARE AND CHURCH GROWTH

Many churches have invested significant sums of money in day care
and nursery school programs in the church facilities on weekdays. In
many instances, the same churches have made extensive provisions
for child care on Sunday mornings and for special parish events and
meetings. Don't overlook the importance of these areas in
contributing to church growth.

1. If your church offers day care, nursery school, or both on a
weekday basis, take advantage of these opportunities by:

- publicizing the provision of these services in your bulletin,
  newsletter, and promotional literature about the church.

- being sure that parish leaders who visit prospective members
  are aware of the services which your church offers.

- asking the day care or nursery school program to be sure
  that participating parents are aware of the church's
  support of the program (at least through the provision

of inexpensive physical facilities and often in more substantial ways).

• having the pastor, other professional staff, or church volunteers lead periodic seminars or workshops for interested parents of day care or nursery school children. This gives positive contact with church leadership (without conflict in the event your day care receives federal monies).

• letting day care and nursery school parents know that the pastor is available for counseling when needed.

• seeing that parents automatically receive the parish newsletter.

Remember that young adult parents may not see immediate connection between the day care or nursery school and the church unless you specifically work to show the connection. When parents see that the church helps with child care because of the church's concern for children, their image of the church will be more positive. Many churches find that keeping church staff members in informal contact with the day care and nursery school results in substantial new members for the church without any conflict for families that already have a different church home but choose to use your weekday child care services.

2. If your church is not already doing so, be sure that child care is provided at parish committee, council, and board meetings and also at the time of study and social groups. Some parishes take a very conservative policy in this regard and only provide the child care during meetings or classes when parents have requested that in advance. The problem with this approach is that the responsibility is placed on the parents, who may already feel uncomfortable about utilizing the church's service in this way. But if your parish seriously wants young adults, including young parents, involved in the church, then child care provision becomes a necessity. Volunteers can provide much of that care, but the cost of paid sitters if needed will be more than repaid by the higher involvement of young parents.

Parents of small children must deal not only with the cost of child care in order to attend church meetings but also with the frequent difficulty of finding qualified persons to provide that care. When the church provides that care, parents receive the clear message that both they and their children are wanted at the church.

18

How Important Is Church Growth?

Go therefore and make disciples of all nations, baptizing them in the name of the Father and of the Son and of the Holy Spirit, teaching them to observe all I have commanded you; and lo, I am with you always, to the close of the age.
Matthew 28:19-20

A bishop of a major Protestant denomination preached passionately to a regional meeting: "We can no longer afford to ignore the issue of church growth. We have for too long manufactured rationalizations for our declining membership and taken refuge in our social action and mission programs. My friends, those programs are important, and I am thoroughly committed to them. But if we continue to decline at our present rate, there will one day no longer be a church to support those worthy causes. We will cease to exist.

"The issue, however, is more than institutional survival. We have been called by Christ to win others to the faith. How will we account to our Lord for the repeated losses in membership which we have sustained? Those are institutional losses but they reflect our failure to share the faith. The time is upon us to take seriously our commission to spread the faith, to win others for the cause of Christ."

A pastor who listened with appreciation to the sermon commented afterwards: "He's right in a way, but is winning others to the faith really the most important task of the church? I remember the church the Bishop pastored in the sixties. There were major racial problems in the community, and he took some strong stands from the pulpit of that church. He lost a lot of members who didn't agree with what he thought the Gospel said about civil rights. Was church growth so important that he should have restrained himself from speaking our against obvious wrong? I don't think church growth is the most important task of the church. I think faithfulness to the Gospel is most important."

A lay person listening to the pastor responded: "We aren't losing members in our congregations because we're taking strong stands on civil rights or anything else. We're losing members because we don't follow up on people who visit our church, and we don't know how to witness to our own faith. We don't sponsor evangelism crusades or revivals. We're content to drift along, living with a little membership loss each year."

A member of another denomination had yet another perspective: "My church, my whole denomination in fact, is gaining members fairly rapidly. We take witnessing to the faith seriously, and we get big attendance at a couple of annual crusades we sponsor. Our problem is what happens once we gain people as members. Lots of our members drift into inactivity very quickly. We don't do a good job helping people grow in the faith, and we may push a little too hard for that initial commitment to Christ and the church. I suppose you can't really push too hard for that, but we don't seem to help people grow very well. How much good does it do to get new members and let them become inactive? We need to nurture those people."

All four persons raise valid points, and I'm not prepared to argue that any of them are entirely right or entirely wrong in what they say. The bishop was issuing a needed challenge to the clergy and laity of the churches for which he is responsible. While institutional survival shouldn't be the primary motivation for winning people to Christ and the church, he's right about the validity of the concern. He's also right that sharing the faith with others is an integral part of being a Christian.

Yet I don't believe the bishop would moderate his stand on civil rights in order to protect church growth, and I don't believe he would approve of a pastor doing that. There are situations in which the frank preaching of the Gospel will alienate others, but the Gospel still must be preached.

likewise it seems tragic to win people as church members and then fail to nurture them properly. We are all at various stages in spiritual growth, and one of our most important functions in the church is to nourish that growth. We don't want to be like the Pharisees whom Jesus criticized for winning converts only to make them twice as fit for hell as they themselves already were (Matthew 23:15)!

I believe church growth is important. I also believe many of our churches have needlessly neglected the things that make for church growth. Most of those things are also basic to good pastoral care and the nurture of people. Too many of us have become sloppy and complacent as church communities – perhaps a little too satisfied with things as they are. We need new challenge to reach out to others, and we need to develop new habits and procedures which will help our churches grow.

Our ministries, however, must be wholistic. We must be concerned, as Christ was concerned, with the total well-being of individuals, the church, and the community. We cannot neglect witness to human rights and world peace because we want our churches to grow and don't want to risk being unpopular. We must not fail to nurture the people who are in our churches. We need quality Christian education, meaningful church community activities, good pastoral care, and opportunities for service to others.

Christ works through us and at times even in spite of us. We do not always know the answers to all the dilemmas which confront us. I think of the eloquent words of José María Arguedas:

Is not what we know far less that the great hope we feel?[1]

We do not have all the answers, and our response to the needs around us will always be imperfect for we are imperfect people in an imperfect world. We serve one who is perfect and who always gives us reason to hope.

We must in each situation make the best witness we can for our Lord – as individuals and as religious communities. The rest must be trusted to God.

A pastor named Ben Garrison took very strong civil rights stands in a midwestern community in the late sixties. Many of his positions were unpopular, and he did lose members. I was a young college student in his congregation at that time, and I will never forget the force of his words and their positive impact on the lives of many people. The church members he lost found new church homes, and there are people who had ignored the church for years who were drawn by his powerful, uncompromising witness. One young college student decided to enter seminary in large part because of that man's courage in the name of Christ. That college student many years later wrote a book on church growth.

[1] "Ultimo Diario?" in *Obras Completas*. Lima: Horizonte, 1983, 5:197

19

Thirty Day Experiment and Study Guide

For where two or three are gathered in my name, there am I in the midst of them.

Matthew 18: 20

I firmly believe that you and I can make a difference in church growth:

• One person, working alone, can share the faith with others and cause others to join the Christian community as it is made known in the institutional church. One person can help change the attitudes of others in the church in ways that will create greater possibilities for church growth.

• Two or three people working together can share prayer, ideas, and emotional support which will enrich their efforts for church growth.

• Significant numbers of people in a local church who are committed to sharing the good news of Jesus Christ can truly, by God's grace, bring about enormous growth in the local church.

This chapter invites you to join with others in a thirty day experiment in church growth. The thirty days include five days on which you meet as a group to discuss the situation in your parish and the experiences which you are having. The other twenty-five days involve you in prayer, study, research, and action related to church growth and to the enrichment of your own faith. Space has been provided for you to record what you accomplish and your reflections on those accomplishments in journal writing style.

The "group" you ask to work with you for the thirty day experiment may be one, two, or three close friends who also share concern about the Christian faith and the local church. The group may be a Fishers' Club or evangelism committee in the church. The group may be an adult Sunday school class, a short term interest group, a prayer group, a staff group, the parish council or administrative board, or another church organization.

Thirty days will not solve all the problems of your parish. Thirty days may not be long enough for you to actually bring one new person into parish membership. But it is long enough for you to grow in your commitment to parish growth, for you to influence some others in your church, and for you to start sharing your faith with others in significant ways.

The first day of the experiment involves reading the first and second chapters of this book in anticipation of group discussion on the second day. Be sure that copies of the book are available to group members before the first day of the experiment.

DAY ONE: Read chapters one and two of *Plain Talk About Church Growth*. Then complete the sentences which follow in your own words:

1. I think that most people who join our church do so because

2. I would like to share my faith with others and invite others to come to church, but I am sometimes blocked because

3. It would be easier for me to reach out to others in the name of Christ if

DAY TWO: FIRST GROUP MEETING

Prior to the meeting, one person should obtain from the church office the record of church membership and average worship attendance for the last ten years. If possible, make copies of this information for group members. Have available the names and addresses of some people who have visited your church over the last one to three months. Put each name on a separate card, so these can be given to group members for their use during the coming week. You may want to share light refreshments at the end of each group meeting. Have refreshments available for this meeting, and also recruit volunteers to provide them for the four future meetings.

Step One. Open with a time of prayer, asking God's presence with the group during your meeting. Read and share refections on Matthew 28: 19-20.

Step Two. Go around the group, letting each person respond. If you do not all know one another, each person should share his or her name. Then share what you would each be doing at this time if you had not decided to be part of the "Thirty Day Experiment." This should help you understand that you are together because of common commitment and concern about the church.

Step Three: Share your responses to the three sentences which were completed privately on the first day of the experiment. If you have not all had opportunity to complete those sentences, take a few minutes of group time to do so. Ask questions of one another as you need to clarify responses.

Step Four. Look at the information which has been collected about your church's membership and average attendance over the past ten years. Share your observations about what has happened in the growth or decline of your neighborhood or city population during that same period of time.

Step Five. Share your reflections about the seven observations on "Church Growth in North America" which are in the first chapter. Share which of the observations seem most important and why. If you disagree with any of the observations, talk about your reasons. If you had to add two new observations related to your own church and community, what would those be?

Step Six. The leader should give a card with the name and address of a visitor to your church to each member of the group. If there are not enough cards for each member of the group, then work together to identify the names of other persons in your community who might be prospective members. During the coming week, you will all be visiting one of the persons who has visited your church or who has been identified as a prospective member.

Step Seven. Close with prayer, asking God's support for each person in the group in the week ahead. Ask God to guide and direct you as you seek to involve others in the church. Give God thanks for the opportunity to share together.

DAY THREE: Don't delay! Use today to make a visit to the visitor or prospective member who was assigned to you. Tell that person you are sharing in a group that wants to share Christ "s love and help your church grow. Explain that you want to better understand the factors that cause a person to want to join a local church or that cause a person not to join a local church. Ask that person to share with you his or her impressions about your church. Respond with your own observations, but don't be defensive if the person is critical of some factors about your church. Record your refections on the experience in the space below.

If you are unable to see that person (or family) today, then make an appointment to do so later in the week. It's important to get started! If you feel uncomfortable about making the first visit by yourself, ask someone else in the group to go with you.

DAY FOUR: Read chapter three. Record your own observations about this concept from the chapter:

When people lead prosperous lives and at least appear successful, they may miss the importance of sharing Christ's love with others.

DAY FIVE: Visit with someone who has been a member of your church longer than you have – preferably someone who is one of the oldest members of the church. (If you are personally one of the oldest members of the church, then visit with someone else who has been a member about the same length of time.) Don't choose someone who is sharing with you in the Thirty Day Experiment. It's fine to have the visit by telephone if that "s the most convenient approach. Ask that person to share his or her reflections on the growth and/or decline in church membership. Ask that person what factors have seemed to attract people to the church and keep people away from the church. Ask that person to share what changes he or she has seen in the church as new members have been added. Record the comments of that person and your own observation.

DAY SIX: Read chapter four, including the marketing questions. Write out your answers to the first twelve marketing questions. Use the space provided in that chapter or separate sheets of paper if you need more room. Your written responses don't have to be detailed, but you should give careful thought to each of the questions. Record on this page the major strengths and weaknesses of your church which you identified in responding to those twelve questions.

DAY SEVEN: Write out your answers to the last twelve marketing questions in chapter four. Use the space provided in that chapter or separate sheets of paper if you need more room. Your written responses don "t have to be detailed, but you should give careful thought to each of the questions. Don't complete the spaces in chapter four for recording the overall strengths and weaknesses of your church; you'll do that as a group. Record on this page the major strengths and weaknesses of your church which you identified in responding to the last twelve questions of chapter four.

DAY EIGHT: Take the CHURCH GROWTH QUIZ which follows. Think about ways you might use copies of his quiz to inform other church leaders about the importance of church growth and about meaningful strategies for church growth. Your reading in this book should make the quiz easier for you than for others with whom you may share it.

CHURCH GROWTH QUIZ

You have permission to reproduce this quiz and the answers for use in your parish, at the denominational level, or in any other way that will be useful to you. Please give credit to Brethren Press and include our address on copies which you make: Brethren Press, 1451 Dundee Avenue, Elgin, illinois 60120. Answers and brief explanations follow the quiz.

1. Approximately what percentage of Americans claim that they are members of a local church?

(a) 50% (b) 60% (c) 70% (d) 80% (e) 90%

2. Approximately what percentage of Americans can be accurately described as "highly spiritually committed?

(a) 10% (b) 20% (c) 30% (d) 40%

3. What percentage of American teens believe you can be a good

Christian and not go to church?

(a) 10% (b) 25% (c) 50% (d) 5%

4.   What percentage of those persons who are "highly spiritually committed" would describe themselves as being "very happy"?

(a) 30% (b) 50%   (c) 70% (d) 90%

5.   Women are more likely than men to have confidence in the church as an institution and to be active in its programs.

(a) True (b) False

6.   Young adults (18-34 years of age) have gone through a transition and are now more likely than older adults to be active in the life of a church.

(a) True (b) False

7.   The best way to follow up on a break in worship, class, or group attendance by a young person or an adult is with a

(a) phone call (b) letter (c) personal visit

8.   The best way to follow up on a visitor to worship who could be a prospective member is with a

(a) phone call (b) letter (c) personal visit

9.   According to Gallup polls, approximately what percentage of teenagers would respond positively if invited to a weekend spiritual life retreat?

(a) 25% (b) 33% (c) 40% (d) 50% (e) 60%

10.   Young adults (18-34 years of age) are most likely to disagree with older adults over

(a)   the divinity of Christ.

(b) the importance of regular church attendance.

(c) the place of prayer in the Christian life.

(d) sexual values.

(e) none of the above.

11. The average first visit to the home of a prospective member needs to be about how many minutes in length.

(a) 10   (b) 20 (c) 30 (d) 60 (e) 75

12. The single greatest reason people give for joining a particular local congregation is

(a) their positive feelings for the pastor.

(b) the encouragement of a friend or neighbor.

(c) the location of the church.

(d) the religious education program of the church.

(e) the denomination of the church.

13. If a young person or adult breaks attendance at worship services, a class, or a group, a phone call or a visit within four to six weeks of that break has what percentage of chance of reactivating that person.

(a) 90   (b) 80 (c) 70 (d) 60 (e) 50

14. Some churches do not grow because the potential involvement of new members is threatening to the present members.

(a) True (b) False

15. In general, large growing churches have a larger percentage of members who are more deeply committed to Christ than churches which are not growing.

(a) True (b) False

16. All other things being equal, churches led by well paid pastors tend to grow more rapidly than churches led by less well paid pastors.

(a) True (b) False

17. Some churches are in geographical locations which make growth almost impossible.

(a) True (b) False

ANSWERS TO CHURCH GROWTH QUIZ

1. **(c) 70%.** The percentage is highest in the midwest (74%) and the south (72%) and lowest in the west (58%).

2. **(a) 10%.** The exact percentage who could be described as highly spiritually committed is 12%. These persons are faithful in worship attendance, charitable giving, church involvement service to others, and prayer. Growth in spiritual commitment of members should be a major goal of every parish.

3. **(d) 75%.** 74% of Protestant teens and 82% of Catholic teens feel you can be a good Christian and not go to church. This is reason for concern, because these young people will shape the future of the church. Actual worship attendance by teens is about as high as for adults; but once teens are no longer under strong parental influence, the attendance figure drops dramatically.

4. **(c) 70%.** Those who are "highly spiritually committed" are much more likely to describe themselves as "very happy" than are those of less commitment. Indeed, for the highly uncommitted, the percentage drops to 30%. That says something about the overall life view which the Christian faith has to offer!

5. **(a) True.** Women arc definitely more likely than men to have confidence in the church and to be active in its program. AND, teenagers and young adults tend to accept that role model.
6. **(b) False.** Young adults are reflecting slightly more traditional values than a few years ago, but they are still significantly less likely than older adults to be active in the church.

7. **(a) Phone call.** Letters are generally not successful and may be

misinterpreted as critical. A personal visit may be overreacting if the break in attendance has been a short one. A casual but sincere phone call expressing interest is three times more likely to succeed than a letter. If that doesn't work, try a personal visit.

8. **(c) Personal visit.** When someone has visited worship services, then a personal visit is by far the best option. This makes an extremely positive impression on most potential members. (Of course, some visitors to worship services are excluded as potential members because they are people on vacation or have told you that they are satisfied members of another parish. A letter or card to these persons is an appropriate way to thank them for having worshipped with you and generally makes a positive impression.)

9. **(d) 50%.** 46% of teenage boys and 57% of teenage girls would respond positively if invited to participate in a spiritual life retreat. These figures have remained high for the last several years, yet most churches have not tried spiritual life retreats as a means of outreach. Single young adults show the same interest.

10. **(d) sexual values.** While young adults are not as likely as older adults to have strong commitment to the church the biggest difference comes in sexual values. Young adults, taken as a whole, differ radically from older adults in views of premarital intercourse, abortion, birth control, and divorce. Tensions over those views do keep may young adults out of the church. Dealing with this is difficult but also important.

11. **(a) 10.** Ten minutes is about the right length of time to visit with a prospective member the first time. A longer visit is usually not appropriate until further interest has been expressed. Sometimes a two or three minute visit at the front door can be very effective.

12. **(b). The encouragement of a friend or neighbor.** This is the number one factor in causing people to choose a particular "church home." All the other factors listed, however, are important.

13. **(a) 90%.** Depending on age, the actual range is 89% to 94%. The single most effective step most parishes can take in conserving members and increasing attendance is prompt follow-up on absences. When churches wait six months, the figure drops to 24%-32%.

14. **(a) True.** Many church members are happy with the life of the

church as it is. Growth in membership brings changes to the church and sharing of power and decisions. Those realities can be threatening to some members and cause them not to respond to prospective members in ways that make for church growth.

15. **(b) False.** Members in growing churches are not necessarily more committed to Christ than members of churches which are not growing. Many other factors are involved - including demographics. Some limited research does, however, support the view that the highly committed members in growing churches are more comfortable talking about their faith and the church than the highly committed members in churches which are not growing.

16. **(a) True.** While the salary paid the pastor is obviously not a major determinant in church growth, it is true that, all other things being equal, a church with a better paid pastor is more likely to grow. Why? First better paid pastors are happier with their work and the church – and they reflect that. Second, better paid pastors have longer tenures in the same church and long tenure generally helps church growth. Third, there is an overall relationship between the competency of the church staff and church growth – a higher salary lets churches attract higher quality staff. This is true for youth workers, Christian educators, and other professional staff as well as clergy.

17. **(b) False.** There are 3,151 counties in the United States. All of those counties have residents who are not affiliated with any local church. There is potential for growth almost anywhere. However, certain fast growing parts of the country obviously have the highest potential.

DAY NINE: SECOND GROUP MEETING

Have available the names and addresses of some inactive members of your parish. Put each name on a separate card, so these can be given to group members for their use during the coming week.

Step One. Open with a time of prayer, asking God's presence with the group during your meeting. Read and share reflections on Revelation 3: 15-1 8.

Step Two Have group members share their experiences from visiting with a prospective member or visitor during the week. Have people share:

- What they learned about how the church is seen by prospective members or visitors.

- What they learned about how to approach a visitor or prospective member.

- How they felt about making the visit.

- What they would do differently if they made the same visit again.

- What their next steps should be in relationship to the visitor or prospective member on whom they called.

Step Three. Look at the marketing questionnaire which appears in chapter four. Take time as a group to:

- Let each person share his or her responses to the two or three questions which were of greatest interest to tat person.

- Share in talking about any questions which members were not certain how to answer.

- Identify as a roup the greatest strengths and weaknesses of your church, completing the listings at the end of the fourth chapter.

- Talk about the kinds of persons most likely and least likely to be attracted to your church.

Step Four. Talk about the CHURCH GROWTH QUIZ. Discuss any of the questions or answers which are of special interest to the group. Then share in identifying ways that the quiz might be constructively used to create greater concern about church growth. Also talk about the reality that, as chapter three discusses, institutional survival alone is not the best reason for reaching out to others.

Step Five. Give group members the cards with the names of inactive members on whom they will call during the week.

Step Six. Close with a time of prayer, seeking God's guidance for the week ahead.

DAY TEN: Read chapter five. List on this page as many different "ports of entry" as you can for your church. "Ports of entry" are the groups or contacts which initially bring prospective members to your church. These may include worship services, classes, groups, and so forth.

DAY ELEVEN: Choose a person with whom you are well acquainted who does NOT belong to your church. Choose someone with whom you are comfortable talking. Visit with that individual, in person or by phone, about your commitment to Christ and the church. Explain to that person that you are in a group which is searching together for ways to help the church grow and that you want to gain greater comfort talking about your personal faith and the church. Ask that person to respond as he or she wishes to what you are saying. This does NOT have to be a prospective member; it can lie someone who is active in another church. The main point is to choose someone whom you are comfortable talking with and who is not a member of your parish. Record your reflections on the experience.

DAY TWELVE: Spend some time thinking about all the persons you know who are not, to your knowledge, members of a local church. List those persons here. Remember that all these are people who are potential members for your church.

DAY THIRTEEN: Visit with the inactive church member whose name you were given at the last group meeting. (Or rather than an individual, you may be visiting with a couple or family.) Explain to that person that you are interested in helping your church grow and that you need help understanding how different members feel about the church. Don't put that person on the spot by saying that you are calling because he or she has not been active. Ask that person to share some of his or her feelings about the church. Record your observations.

DAY FOURTEEN: Read chapter six. Think about the plans which have been made in your own church which have not worked out is intended. Record here the kinds of plans for church growth which you feel would be most likely to succeed in your church.

DAY FIFTEEN: Visit with one of the prospective members you identified on day twelve. You can do the visit by phone or in person. Ask that person if he or she is a member of a local church. If so, then ask that person to share his or her impressions of that church with you. If not then talk with that person about possible involvement in your church. You can approach this on several levels: share with this person your own faith in Christ and what that means for you; share an invitation to attend worship services; or share an invitation to attend a class or social event at the church.

DAY SIXTEEN: THIRD GROUP MEETING

Have available the names and addresses of some church members who are hospitalized, living in a nursing home or sheltered care facility, or confined to their own home by sickness or infirmity. Put each name on a separate card, so these can be given to group members for their use during the coming week.

Step One. Open with a time of prayer, asking God's presence with the group during your meeting. Read and share refections on Matthew 9:37.

Step Two. Have group members begin sharing the names of prospective members which they wrote down on day twelve. Put these on chalkboard or newsprint as they are called out. Indicate on how many different lists the same name appears. If group members identify additional prospective members during this process, write those down as well. Assign to each person a prospective member from the list for continued contact. This may be the same person they have already seen at least one time.

Step Three. Have group members share refections on the calls which they made during the week. Have them share what went well; what went poorly; what they would do differently another time.

Step Four. Have group members share their reflections on the kinds of plans for church growth which would be most likely to be successful for your parish. Talk about the concepts given in chapter six as they relate to your own church.

Step Five. Assign each group member a person who is hospitalized, living in a nursing home or sheltered care facility, or confined to home by sickness or infirmity. Talk about the importance of reaching out to these persons as well as to prospective members. Also talk about the ways in which the church's care of persons who are sick or hospitalized helps shape the image of the church.

Step Six. Close with a time of prayer, seeking God's help in the week ahead.

DAY SEVENTEEN: Read chapter seven. Write down the steps you think should be included in a comprehensive calling plan that was designed to reach active members, inactive members, and prospective members in your parish. Include calls by volunteers and staff.

DAY EIGHTEEN: Visit the prospective member you were assigned during the previous session. Your approach will depend on whether or not you have talked to this person previously. Write down your reflections on the experience.

DAY NINETEEN: Read chapter ten. Then go through the yellow pages in your telephone directory. See which churches are listed, and evaluate the advertisements by the standards suggested in chapter eight. Record here your major ideas on better using the media for outreach in your community.

DAY TWENTY: Listen to a popular radio evangelist or watch a popular television evangelist. Compare the messages to the approach of your local church. Try to list five advantages television evangelists have over local churches in reaching the public then list five disadvantages under which media evangelists must work.

DAY TWENTY-ONE: Visit the person who has been confined to his or her own home, a nursing home or sheltered care facility, or a hospital; this would be the person whose name you were given at the third group meeting. Simply explain that you are calling on behalf of the church and want to share your concern for that person's welfare. Ask how things are going and if there is anything you can do to be helpful. Offer to share a prayer with that person before leaving; the Lord's Prayer is appropriate if you are not comfortable sharing an individual prayer. Record your refections on the experience. Was this harder or easier than calling on a prospective member?

DAY TWENTY-TWO: Read chapter eight. If your church is a small one, you may not have any need for additional employed staff. If your church is medium sized or larger, there is a good probability that you could benefit from a larger employed staff. Write down your own observations about the staffing needs (employed and volunteer) of your parish as they related to church growth.

DAY TWENTY-THREE: FOURTH GROUP MEETING

Have available the names and addresses of some people who have visited your church or who have been previously identified as prospective members. Have each name on a separate card, so these can be given to group members for their use during the coming week.

Step One. Open with a time of prayer, asking God's presence with the group during your meeting. Read and share reflections on Acts 6:1-3.

Step Two. Have group members share their experiences from making calls in the previous week. Make decisions together about what future contacts should be made with the prospective members that people in your group have seen.

Step Three. Think about the categories of persons on whom calls or visits are often made. Talk as a group about the differences and similarities in visiting:

- active members of the church
- inactive members of the church
- people who have visited a worship service or a group or activity in your church
- people who are prospective members but who have not visited your church
  - persons who are confined to their homes, nursing homes or sheltered care facilities, or hospitals

Talk together about ways of improving visitation and outreach programs for your parish.

Step Four. Identify what, if anything, your church should do differently in its use of:

- the yellow pages
- newspaper ads

- radio
- network television
- cable television

Step Five. Talk about any staffing additions (employed or volunteer) which group members feel are needed by your parish.

Step Six. Give anyone who will not be continuing to contact a prospective member already assigned the name of a new visitor or prospective member.

Step Seven. Seek God's help in the lives of group members during the week ahead.

DAY TWENTY-FOUR: Read chapter twelve. Go through the list of SMALL THINGS that count in that chapter. Record here areas related to worship in which you feel your church could improve.

DAY TWENTY-FIVE: Make a call on a prospective member or visitor to worship. This may be someone on whom you've called in a previous week, or it may be someone assigned to you at the last group meeting.

DAY TWENTY-SIX: Read chapter thirteen, giving careful attention to the guidelines for new groups. Then record here the new groups which you think should be considered in your parish. Write down one or two reasons for beginning each group that you list.

DAY TWENTY-SEVEN: Call someone who is active in your church and with whom you are well acquainted. Share one or two of your ideas for improving the worship experience in your church (from the perspective of prospective members) or for starting a new group. Ask that person to respond to your ideas. Also ask that person for additional suggestions related to your ideas.

DAY TWENTY-EIGHT: Read chapter fourteen. Record in this space your own reflections on the passage of Scripture with which that chapter begins, Philippians 3: 12-14. How does that passage relate to your own life? To the life of your parish?

DAY TWENTY-NINE: Take time to reflect on the experiences you have had on your own and in cooperation with others during this study. What have you gained from these experiences? What help do you still need to reach out to others more effectively? What directions should your parish take in its efforts to grow?

DAY THIRTY: FIFTH GROUP MEETING

Have available a good quantity of index cards with names and addresses of visitors, prospective members, inactive members, and active members who might especially benefit from a home visit.

Step One. Open with a prayer, asking God's presence with the group during your meeting. Take a few minutes for group members to share their reflections on Philippians 3: 12-14.

Step Two. Take time as a group to go through the check-list in chapter 12 on worship. Identify those areas in which there is strong agreement that improvements are needed. Decide what group in your parish should receive those recommendations.

Step Three. Have group members share their feelings about new classes or groups which are needed in the parish. List the ideas of everyone present, and then try to identify the areas of greatest common concern. Decide on the next steps which should be taken in order to start one or more new groups.

Step Four. Share your experiences in calling on visitors or prospective members. Then decide as a group what continuing programs would help meet the need of reaching out with home visitation in your parish. If people decide to continue making calls as individuals, then be prepared to share the additional cards which have been prepared for the session.

Step Five. Close with a time of open prayer in which each person may share the joys and concerns which have grown from the time spent meeting and studying over the past thirty days. Close by sharing the Lord's Prayer.

And remember that you can personally benefit from reading the remaining chapters in this book, even though those chapters were not specifically assigned for study purposes during the past thirty days.